The UK Ninja Combi Multicooker

Cookbook for Beginners

100 Flavourful and Simple Recipes to Combi Meals, Combi Crisp, Air Fry, Sear/Sauté and More

Colour Edition

George Crouch

TABLE OF CONTENT

INTRODUCTION..1

Chapter 1: Mastering the Ninja Combi Multicooker 3

Benefits of the Ninja Combi Multicooker 4
Control Panel 4
Important Accessories 5
How to Use the Ninja Combi Multicooker ... 6

Essential Cooking Tips.................................. 8
Cleaning and Maintenance 9
FAQs.. 10

Chapter 2: Hearty Breakfasts 11

Baked Beans on Toast 11
Classic Full English Breakfast 11
Grilled Cheese and Ham Toastie 12
Traditional British Scones 12
Breakfast Porridge 13
Avocado and Egg Toast 13

Slow Cooked Breakfast Casserole 14
Toad in the Hole... 14
Grilled Bacon and Tomato Sandwich 15
Rice Pudding 15
Sausage and Mushroom Breakfast Casserole ... 16
Vegetarian Breakfast Hash........................ 16

Chapter 3: Luscious Lunches 17

Beef Steak and Spinach Pasta 17
Salmon and Leek with Quinoa 17
Chicken Alfredo Pasta 18
Lamb Kofta and Couscous......................... 18
Beef and Broccoli Meal.............................. 19
Spaghetti Bolognese 19

Mussels and Garlic Pasta 20
Chicken and Pesto Pasta 20
Thai Red Curry with Tofu and Rice............. 21
Pork Chop and Pumpkin Linguine 21
Pea and Ham Rice Pilaf 22
Creamy Tomato and Basil Rice................... 22

Chapter 4: Dinner Pleasures 23

Salmon and Spinach Risotto 23
Creamy Seafood Pasta 23
Beef and Mushroom Stroganoff with Egg
   Noodles 24
Vegetable Mac and Cheese 24
Sweet and Sour Pork with Rice 25
Prawn and Tomato Pasta 25

Lemon and Herb Rice Pilaf......................... 26
Meatball and Peppers Pasta 26
Chicken and Pea Risotto 27
Spicy Chilli Rice 27
Grilled Lamb Steak with Basil Pasta 28
Mediterranean Chicken with Couscous 28

Chapter 5: Sunday Roasts & Mains...29

Stuffed Chicken Breast with Spinach and
   Feta... 29
Herb-Crusted Leg of Lamb 29
Crispy Duck Breast with Orange Sauce.......... 30
Grilled Rib-eye Steak with Garlic Butter 30
Bangers and Mash with Onion Gravy 31
Seared Pork Tenderloin with Apple and
   Sage 31

Sticky Chicken Thighs with Honey and
   Mustard 32
Beef and Ale Stew...................................... 32
Grilled Halloumi and Vegetable Skewers ... 33
Traditional Lamb Hotpot............................ 33
Beef Brisket with Horseradish Sauce 34
Classic Roast Chicken with Root
   Vegetables.. 34

Chapter 6: Seasonal Vegetables & Sides 35

Roasted Asparagus with Lemon and Parmesan 35
Steamed Garlic Butter Broccoli 35
Crispy Parmesan Courgettes 36
Roasted Pumpkin with Sage and Nutmeg ... 36
Chickpea and Spinach Stir-Fry 37
Mustard Cauliflower with Cheddar 37

Beetroot with Feta and Walnuts 38
Creamy Potato and Leek Soup 38
Honey Glazed Roast Carrots with Mustard Seeds 39
Thyme Sweet Potato Wedges 39
Steamed Minted New Potatoes 40
Buttery Mushrooms with Garlic and Thyme ... 40

Chapter 7: Seafood Specialties 41

Steamed Lemon Herb Salmon 41
Grilled Prawn Skewers with Lime and Coriander 41
Battered Prawns with Garlic Mayonnaise ... 42
Lobster Tails with Herbed Butter 42
Mussels in Garlic Butter 43
Grilled Garlic Oysters with Parsley 43

Salmon Stir-Fry with Asparagus and Spinach 44
Crab Cakes with Lemon and Dill 44
Grilled Whole Trout with Lemon 45
Traditional Steamed Haddock with Peas ... 45
Baked Cod with Parsley Crust 46
Chilli Scallops with Coriander 46

Chapter 8: Celebration Feasts 47

Classic Scotch Eggs 47
Festive Mince Pies 47
Grilled Beef Burgers with Cheddar Cheese ... 48
Pigs in Blankets 48
Steak and Kidney Pie 49
Fish and Chips 49
Lamb Chops with Garlic and Thyme 50

Stuffing Balls 50
Crispy Pork Belly with Apple Sauce 51
Lemon Drizzle Cake 51
Mini Yorkshire Puddings 52
Classic Shepherd's Pie 52
Beef Wellington Bites 53
Classic British Vegetable Stew 53

Chapter 9: Savoury Snacks 54

Cheese and Onion Pasties 54
Breadcrumbs Stuffed Mushrooms 54
Spicy Crispy Chickpeas 55
Cheesy Cauliflower Bites 55
Mini Fishcakes 56
Garlic Potato Wedges with Rosemary 56

Crispy Fish Fingers 57
Garlic Mushrooms 57
Homemade Chicken Goujons 58
Mushroom Arancini 58
Cheese and Chive Potato Bake 59
Mini Sausage Rolls 59

Chapter 10: Dessert Delights 60

Apple and Cinnamon Cake 60
Banoffee Pie 60
Carrot and Walnut Cake 61
Homemade Bread Rolls 61
Sticky Toffee Pudding 62
Gingerbread Cake 62

Chocolate Chip Cookies 63
Homemade Apple Crumble 63
Victoria Sponge Cake 64
Cinnamon Buns 64
Treacle Tart 65
Fruit Loaf Cake 65

Appendix 1: Measurement Conversion Chart 66

Appendix 2: Recipes Index 67

INTRODUCTION

Welcome to your new favourite kitchen companion! As someone who loves cooking but values efficiency, I couldn't be more thrilled to share this Ninja Combi Multicooker guide with you. Whether you're a seasoned chef or a complete beginner, this versatile appliance is here to simplify your mealtimes while keeping the flavour and fun intact.

The Ninja Combi isn't just an appliance; it's like having an extra pair of hands in the kitchen. It combines the power of a multi-cooker, oven, and air fryer, offering you endless possibilities. From steaming rice and baking fluffy cakes to air-frying crispy chips and preparing perfectly balanced one-pot meals, this machine does it all.

When I first started using the Ninja Combi, I was amazed by how intuitive it was. With features like the SmartSwitch and its range of modes, I could seamlessly switch between slow cooking a hearty stew and crisping up golden roast potatoes. It's a game-changer, especially for busy households or those who love experimenting with new recipes.

In this cookbook, I'll take you through everything you need to know—from understanding the basics of your Ninja Combi to whipping up delicious meals with ease. The recipes are designed with UK kitchens in mind, featuring familiar ingredients and straightforward steps. I've made sure to include tips and tricks that will help you get the best results, whether you're steaming vegetables or perfecting a Sunday roast.

Cooking should never feel like a chore, and with the Ninja Combi, it truly doesn't. Let's dive in and discover how to make mealtimes quicker, tastier, and more enjoyable.

So, pop the kettle on, and let's get started!

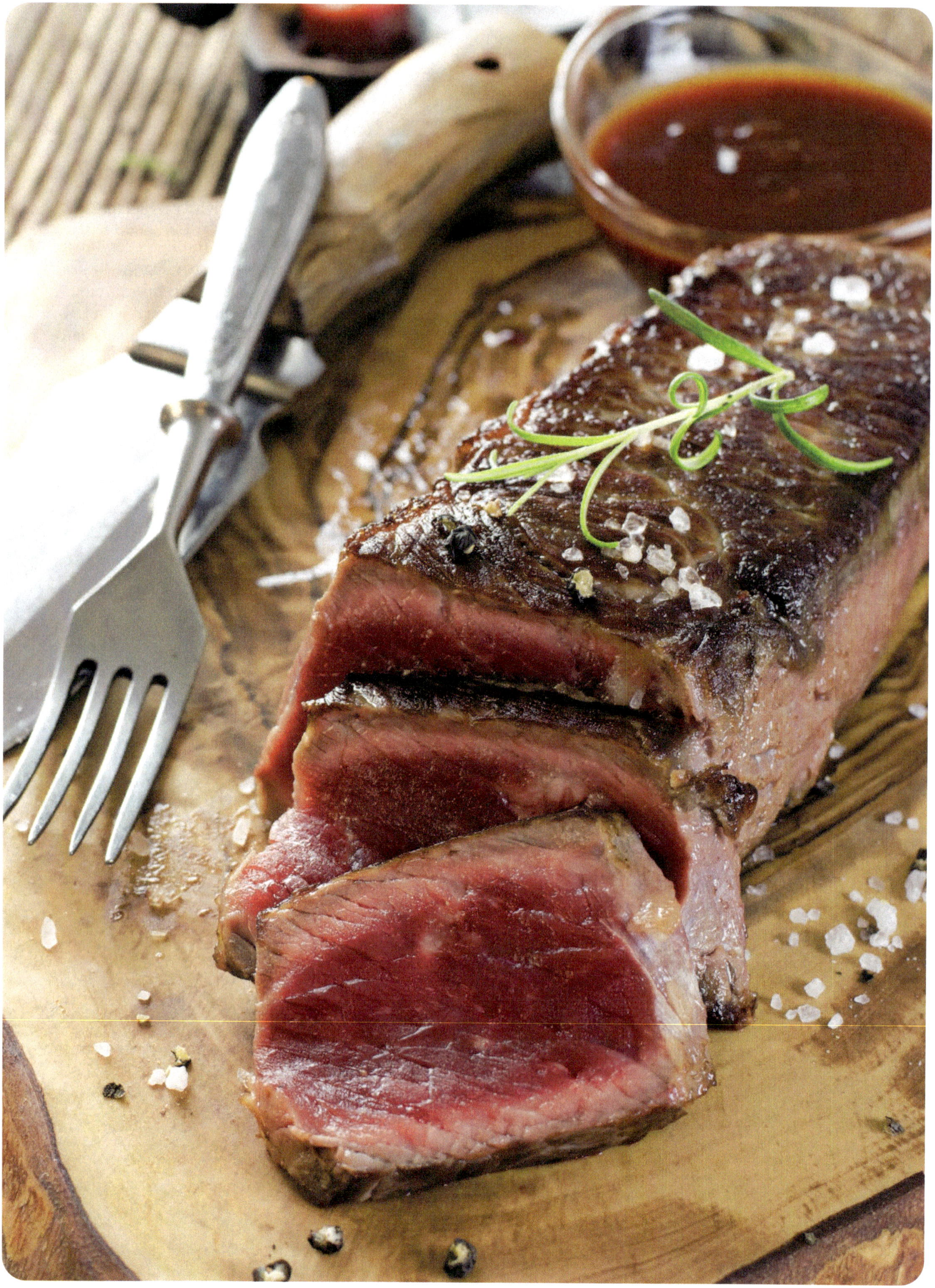

CHAPTER 1: MASTERING THE NINJA COMBI MULTICOOKER

The Ninja Combi Multicooker is an innovative kitchen appliance designed to make mealtimes easier and more versatile. It combines the functionality of a multi-cooker, air fryer, grill and slow cooker in one compact unit, allowing you to create a wide variety of meals with ease. From hearty stews and steamed vegetables to crispy chips and golden roasts, the Ninja Combi delivers exceptional results while saving time and effort.

At the heart of the Ninja Combi is its SmartSwitch technology, which allows you to switch seamlessly between Combi Cooker and Air Fry/Hob modes. This gives you access to a range of cooking functions, including steaming, slow cooking, air frying, grilling, and baking. Each function is optimised for consistent performance, and the simple controls make it easy to set cooking times and temperatures for perfect results every time.

The Ninja Combi's two-level cooking system is a standout feature, enabling you to prepare complete meals in one go. You can cook grains or pasta in the bottom pan while roasting proteins or vegetables on the top tray. This not only saves time but also reduces washing up, making it ideal for busy households or anyone looking to prepare balanced meals quickly and conveniently.

Designed with efficiency in mind, the Ninja Combi ensures even and reliable cooking. Its powerful heating elements work together to deliver consistent results, whether you're roasting a chicken, baking a cake, or crisping up sweet potato fries. The appliance is also versatile enough to handle everything from quick midweek meals to more elaborate weekend dishes, adapting effortlessly to your cooking needs.

Compact and thoughtfully designed for UK kitchens, the Ninja Combi is both practical and stylish. Its spacious interior can cater for family meals or smaller portions, while its compatibility with UK ingredients and metric measurements ensures a hassle-free cooking experience. Whether you're an experienced cook or just starting out, the Ninja Combi Multicooker is a reliable and adaptable addition to any kitchen.

Benefits of the Ninja Combi Multicooker

The Ninja Combi Multicooker is packed with features that make it an indispensable addition to any kitchen. Here are seven key benefits of this versatile appliance:

●*All-in-One Functionality*
The Ninja Combi combines the roles of a multi-cooker, oven, and air fryer in one compact unit. Whether you're roasting, baking, air frying, steaming, or slow cooking, it replaces multiple appliances, saving valuable worktop space.

●*Time-Saving Efficiency*
With its dual-level cooking system, you can prepare complete meals in one go. Cook grains or pasta in the bottom pan while roasting proteins and vegetables on the top tray, cutting down cooking time and washing up.

●*Versatility for Every Meal*
From quick snacks to elaborate family dinners, the Ninja Combi handles it all. Its functions include air frying, steaming, grilling, slow cooking, and baking, giving you the flexibility to create a wide variety of dishes with ease.

●*Simple and Intuitive Controls*
The appliance features SmartSwitch technology, making it effortless to switch between cooking modes. With straightforward time and temperature adjustments, even beginners can achieve excellent results.

●*Compact Yet Spacious Design*
While fitting neatly on most UK kitchen worktops, the Ninja Combi has a generous capacity that's per-

fect for families or meal prepping. You can cook for up to 6-8 people in one cycle, making it ideal for busy households or entertaining guests.

●*Healthier Cooking Options*
The air fry function allows you to create crispy, golden dishes with little to no oil, offering a healthier alternative to traditional frying. It's perfect for making chips, breaded fish, and other favourites without the added guilt.

●*Energy Efficiency*
Compared to traditional ovens, the Ninja Combi uses less energy, helping to reduce your utility bills while delivering faster cooking times. It's a practical choice for those who want to save both time and money in the kitchen.

With these benefits, the Ninja Combi Multicooker makes mealtimes easier, healthier, and more enjoyable, while bringing professional-level results to your everyday cooking.

Control Panel

The Ninja Combi Multicooker features a user-friendly control panel that allows you to manage your cooking effortlessly. With clearly labelled buttons and straightforward settings, it gives you precise control over every meal. Here's an overview of the Cooking Functions and Operating Buttons:

Cooking Functions
Each cooking function is designed to simplify and enhance your experience in the kitchen:

■ Combi Meals: Ideal for preparing proteins, grains, and vegetables simultaneously, creating complete meals in a single cycle.

- Combi Crisp: Perfect for achieving juicy interiors and crispy exteriors, ideal for roasts, root vegetables, and frozen proteins.
- Combi Bake: Excellent for baking fluffy bread, moist cakes, and casseroles with an even texture.
- Steam: Retains moisture, flavour, and nutrients while gently cooking delicate foods like fish or vegetables.
- Rice/Pasta: Prepares no-drain rice or pasta effortlessly for quick and convenient dishes.
- Air Fry: Creates crispy, golden results with little to no oil, suitable for chips, nuggets, and other fried favourites.
- Grill: Uses high heat to caramelise or brown food, such as melting cheese or achieving perfect grill marks.
- Prove: Creates an ideal environment for dough to rise, ensuring successful bread and pastry results.
- Sear/Sauté: Browns meat, sautés vegetables, or simmers sauces with precise heat control.
- Slow Cook: Cooks food gently over a longer period for tender stews, soups, and casseroles.
- Reheat: Warms leftovers gently while maintaining their original texture and flavour.

Operating Buttons

The operating buttons make it easy to navigate through the Ninja Combi's features:

- SmartSwitch: Switches between Combi Cooker and Air Fry/Hob modes. Available functions illuminate automatically based on the selected mode.
- Function Arrows: Located in the centre, these arrows allow you to scroll through the cooking functions and select the one you need.
- Temperature Arrows: Positioned on the left, these arrows let you adjust the temperature to suit your recipe's requirements.
- Time Arrows: Found on the right, these arrows help you set the precise cooking time in one-minute increments.
- Start/Stop Button: Starts the selected cooking function or stops it during operation if adjustments are needed.
- Power Button: Turns the appliance on and off, stopping all ongoing cooking processes.
- Light Button: Illuminates the interior, allowing you to check the progress of your food without interrupting the cooking process.

The Ninja Combi Multicooker offers a wide range of cooking functions and straightforward controls, ensuring every meal is prepared with precision and ease.

Important Accessories

The Ninja Combi Multicooker comes with a range of essential accessories that are designed to enhance your cooking experience. Each accessory is crafted to ensure that your meals, from crispy snacks to full dinners, are cooked to perfection. Here's an overview of the key accessories:

Combi Pan

The non-stick, high-walled Combi Pan is perfect for baking, roasting, and steaming. It can also double as a serving dish, making it ideal for one-pot meals. The Combi Pan is specifically designed to fit perfectly within the Ninja Combi, ensuring even heat distribution for optimal cooking results.

Crisper Plate

The Crisper Plate is used for air frying and crisping your food. It fits inside the Combi Pan, allowing hot air to circulate evenly around your ingredients. This results in a crispy exterior while keeping the inside tender and moist. It's perfect for making crispy chips, roasted vegetables, or frozen snacks with minimal oil.

Bake Tray

The Bake Tray is essential for dishes that need even heat from both the top and bottom, such as roasts or baked goods. Its non-stick surface ensures easy food release, while the tray's design maximises airflow, giving you that golden, crisp finish you desire.

Each of these accessories works seamlessly with the Ninja Combi, making your cooking process easier, more efficient, and delivering the best results. Proper care and maintenance of these accessories will extend their lifespan and ensure your Ninja Combi continues to perform at its best.

How to Use the Ninja Combi Multicooker

The Ninja Combi Multicooker makes cooking a breeze with its wide array of functions, designed to streamline your kitchen routine while delivering delicious meals. Whether you're preparing a quick weeknight dinner or an elaborate feast, here's how to make the most of each cooking mode:

1.SMARTSWITCH to COMBI COOKER Functions

Combi Meals

This function lets you prepare a complete meal with multiple components at once, perfect for busy families or meal prep.

Steps:
1. Add liquid and ingredients (e.g., rice or pasta with water) to the Combi Pan (Level 1). Place proteins and vegetables on the Bake Tray (Level 2).
2. Slide the Combi Pan into Level 1 and the Bake Tray into Level 2.
3. Flip the SmartSwitch to Combi Cooker and select Combi Meals.
4. Set the temperature and time, then press Start/Stop. The unit will steam for 5-10 minutes before cooking.
5. Once cooking is complete, carefully remove the tray and pan.

Combi Crisp

Achieve crispy textures on meats and vegetables while keeping them tender on the inside.

Steps:
1. Pour the required amount of water into the Combi Pan for steaming and place the Crisper Plate on top.
2. Arrange your food on the Crisper Plate.
3. Slide the Combi Pan into Level 1.
4. Flip the SmartSwitch to Combi Cooker and select Combi Crisp.
5. Set the temperature and cooking time, then press Start/Stop. The unit will steam before crisping.
6. Halfway through, open the door and flip/toss the food, then close the door to continue cooking.

Combi Bake

Perfect for baking bread, cakes, and other baked goods, achieving a light and fluffy texture.

Steps:
1. Pour water into the Combi Pan for steaming.
2. Place your baking ingredients into the Bake Tray or other baking dishes, then slide into Level 2.
3. Slide the Combi Pan into Level 1.
4. Flip the SmartSwitch to Combi Cooker and select Combi Bake.
5. Set the temperature and time, then press Start/Stop. The unit will steam before baking.
6. Once the baking is complete, remove the tray and allow it to cool as needed.

Rice/Pasta

This function lets you cook rice or pasta without the need for draining.

Steps:
1. Add the appropriate amount of water and rice or pasta to the Combi Pan.
2. Slide the Combi Pan into Level 1.
3. Flip the SmartSwitch to Combi Cooker and select Rice/Pasta.
4. The function will default to rice; use the arrows to switch to pasta if needed.
5. Press Start/Stop to begin cooking. Once done, the unit will beep and keep your food warm.

Steam

Ideal for cooking delicate foods, preserving their nutrients and texture.

Steps:
1. Pour water into the Combi Pan and place the Crisper Plate on top.
2. Add your ingredients to the Crisper Plate.
3. Slide the Combi Pan into Level 1.
4. Flip the SmartSwitch to Combi Cooker and select Steam.
5. Set the cooking time and press Start/Stop. This function does not require temperature adjustments.

6. Once complete, remove the pan and food.

Prove
Create the perfect environment for dough to rise.

Steps:
1. Pour water into the Combi Pan for steaming and place the Crisper Plate on top.
2. Place your dough in a cake tin, then slide the tin into the Combi Pan on top of the Crisper Plate.
3. Slide the pan into Level 1.
4. Flip the SmartSwitch to Combi Cooker and select Prove.
5. Set the temperature (20°C to 35°C) and the proving time, then press Start/Stop.
6. Once proving is complete, proceed with baking your dough.

2. SMARTSWITCH to AIR FRY/HOB Functions

Grill
Use high heat to brown and caramelise food, perfect for grilling meats and vegetables.

Steps:
1. Place your ingredients on the Bake Tray and slide it into Level 2.
2. Flip the SmartSwitch to Air Fry/Hob and select Grill.
3. Set the cooking time (there is no temperature adjustment) and press Start/Stop.
4. When cooking is complete, remove the tray and serve.

Air Fry
Get crispy, crunchy food with minimal oil, perfect for chips, chicken, and more.

Steps:
1. Place the Crisper Plate in the Combi Pan and add your ingredients.
2. Slide the Combi Pan into Level 1.
3. Flip the SmartSwitch to Air Fry/Hob and select Air Fry.
4. Set the temperature and cooking time. Remember to add 5 extra minutes for preheating before adding ingredients.
5. When cooking is complete, remove the pan and serve.

Bake
Use dry heat for traditional baking, ideal for cakes, cookies, and pastries.

Steps:
1. Prepare your ingredients and place them in the Bake Tray.
2. Flip the SmartSwitch to Air Fry/Hob and select Bake.
3. Set the temperature and time, then press Start/Stop to begin preheating (it will take around 3 minutes).
4. Once preheating is complete, open the door and slide the tray into Level 1. Close the door to start cooking.
5. When baking is finished, remove the tray and allow it to cool.

Slow Cook
Cook your meals at a low temperature over an extended period, ideal for stews and soups.

Steps:
1. Add your ingredients to the Combi Pan.
2. Flip the SmartSwitch to Air Fry/Hob and select Slow Cook.
3. Set the temperature to HI or LO and choose a cooking time (4-12 hours on HI, 6-12 hours on LO).
4. Press Start/Stop to begin cooking.
5. When the cooking is complete, remove the pan and serve.

Sear/Sauté
This function is perfect for browning meats or sautéing vegetables before cooking.

Steps:
1. Slide the Combi Pan into Level 1.
2. Flip the SmartSwitch to Air Fry/Hob and select Sear/Sauté.
3. Set the temperature and press Start/Stop. The pan will preheat for 2 minutes.
4. Add oil or butter, then your ingredients.
5. Once done, carefully remove the pan and serve.

Reheat
Warm leftovers gently to restore their flavour and texture.

Steps:
1. Place your food in the Combi Pan or on the Crisper Plate.
2. Flip the SmartSwitch to Air Fry/Hob and select Reheat.
3. Set the time and press Start/Stop to begin warming.
4. Once reheating is complete, remove the pan and serve.

With these easy-to-follow steps, you'll be able to explore the full range of the Ninja Combi Multicooker's capabilities, making meal preparation quick, efficient, and enjoyable.

Essential Cooking Tips

To make the most of your Ninja Combi Multicooker, here are some essential cooking tips that will help you achieve the best results every time. Whether you're a seasoned cook or a beginner, these tips will guide you in using the appliance to its full potential.

1. Preheat the Unit
Although many functions on the Ninja Combi don't require preheating, some, like Air Fry and Bake, work best when you allow the unit to preheat for a few minutes before adding your ingredients. This ensures the food starts cooking at the right temperature right away, helping to achieve crispier, more even results.

2. Use the Right Accessories for the Job
The Ninja Combi comes with a variety of accessories, each designed for specific cooking tasks.

Combi Pan: Perfect for one-pot meals, steaming, and cooking grains.
Crisper Plate: Ideal for air frying, crisping, and roasting.
Bake Tray: Best for baking, roasting, and grilling.

Always use the appropriate accessory for the cooking function to get the best texture and cooking performance.

3. Don't Overfill the Pan
To ensure even cooking, it's important not to overfill the Combi Pan or Bake Tray. Overcrowding can prevent hot air from circulating properly, which may result in uneven cooking. For air frying, give your ingredients enough space for the air to circulate, and for steaming, make sure the water level is correct to prevent burning.

4. Shake or Turn Food for Even Crisping
When using the Air Fry or Combi Crisp functions, remember to shake or turn your food halfway through the cooking process. This helps achieve an even, golden crisp on all sides, whether you're making chips, chicken wings, or roasted vegetables.

5. Adjust Cooking Times for Your Ingredients
Cooking times can vary based on the type, size, and cut of your ingredients. If you find that a recipe isn't cooking quite as expected, try adjusting the time or temperature. For example, larger cuts of meat may need a little longer to cook through, while delicate items like fish or certain vegetables may cook faster.

6. Use the Right Liquids for Steaming
When using the Steam function, always ensure there

is enough water in the Combi Pan to create steam. It's important to add the correct amount of liquid to prevent burning the bottom of the pan. Be sure to check your recipe for specific liquid measurements, especially when preparing grains or pasta.

7. Let Food Rest After Cooking

After cooking, particularly for roasted meats or baked goods, let your food rest for a few minutes before serving. This allows the juices in meats to redistribute, ensuring moist and tender results. For baked goods, resting helps set the texture.

8. Clean Regularly for Optimal Performance

To keep your Ninja Combi Multicooker in tip-top condition, make sure to clean it after every use. Wash the Combi Pan, Crisper Plate, and Bake Tray in warm, soapy water, and wipe down the interior of the unit with a damp cloth. Regular cleaning will ensure your appliance continues to perform at its best, and helps avoid the buildup of grease or food residue.

By following these essential tips, you'll be able to make the most of your Ninja Combi Multicooker, ensuring your meals are cooked to perfection every time, with minimal effort and maximum flavour.

Cleaning and Maintenance

To ensure your Ninja Combi Multicooker continues to perform at its best and remains in excellent condition, regular cleaning and proper maintenance are essential. Here's a guide to help you maintain your appliance for long-lasting use:

1. Turn Off and Unplug Before Cleaning

Always turn off the Ninja Combi and unplug it from the power socket before cleaning. Allow the unit to cool down completely to avoid burns or injury. This will also prevent any electrical hazards while cleaning.

2. Clean After Every Use

For the best results, clean the Ninja Combi after every use to prevent food residue from building up. This helps maintain its performance and keeps your meals tasting fresh.

3. Clean the Removable Accessories

➢ Combi Pan, Crisper Plate, and Bake Tray: These accessories are easy to clean and should be washed after each use. Use warm, soapy water and a soft cloth or sponge to remove any food residue. If necessary, soak them for a few minutes before

scrubbing gently.
➢ Non-stick Surfaces: To protect the non-stick coating on these accessories, avoid using abrasive scouring pads or harsh cleaners. A nylon brush or soft sponge will prevent scratching and damage.
➢ Crisper Plate and Bake Tray: For stubborn food residue, you can soak these accessories in warm soapy water to loosen any stuck-on bits before cleaning.

4. Wipe the Interior and Control Panel

After each use, wipe down the interior of the Ninja Combi with a damp cloth to remove any food splashes or spills. The control panel can be cleaned with a soft, dry cloth. Avoid using excessive moisture on the control panel to prevent any damage to the electronics.

5. Clean the Exterior

The exterior of the Ninja Combi should be wiped with a damp cloth to remove fingerprints, grease, and dust. Do not immerse the unit in water, and never use abrasive cleaners that could scratch the surface. For stubborn spots, use a mild dishwashing liquid and a soft cloth.

6. Dry Thoroughly Before Storing

Once all parts are cleaned, dry them thoroughly before storing or reassembling the appliance. This helps prevent any moisture buildup, which could lead to the growth of mould or mildew.

7. Regularly Check for Wear and Tear

Inspect the power cord and plug regularly to ensure there are no signs of wear or damage. If you notice any fraying or exposed wires, discontinue use and contact customer service for assistance. Keeping the power cord in good condition is crucial for safe operation.

8. Storage

When storing your Ninja Combi Multicooker, make sure it's completely dry and free from food residue. Store the appliance in a dry, cool place, away from direct sunlight or heat sources. You can also store the accessories in the unit when not in use to keep everything together and save space.

FAQs

Here are some of the most common questions about the Ninja Combi Multicooker, along with helpful answers to ensure you get the most out of your appliance.

1. Can I use metal utensils in the Ninja Combi?

It is recommended to avoid using metal utensils as they can damage the non-stick coating on the Combi Pan, Crisper Plate, and Bake Tray. Use silicone, wooden, or plastic utensils to protect the surfaces and extend the lifespan of your accessories.

2. How do I prevent food from sticking to the Combi Pan?

To prevent food from sticking, always ensure that you use a small amount of oil or cooking spray when required, particularly for air frying or roasting. For easy cleaning, wash the Combi Pan after each use with warm soapy water, and avoid using harsh scrubbers that can damage the non-stick surface.

3. Can I cook frozen food in the Ninja Combi?

Yes, the Ninja Combi is perfect for cooking frozen food, especially when using the Air Fry or Combi Crisp functions. For best results, no need to thaw the food beforehand—simply follow the recommended cooking time and temperature, adding a few extra minutes for preheating when using the air fry function.

4. Can I cook multiple meals at once?

Yes, the Ninja Combi's dual-level cooking system allows you to prepare multiple components of a meal at the same time. For example, you can cook grains like rice or pasta in the Combi Pan while roasting vegetables or proteins on the Bake Tray. This makes it ideal for preparing complete meals in one go.

5. How do I know which accessory to use for different functions?

Combi Pan: Use for one-pot meals, steaming, and cooking grains.

Crisper Plate: Ideal for air frying, crisping, and roasting.

Bake Tray: Best for baking, roasting, and grilling.

Each accessory is designed to optimise the cooking function it's used with, so refer to your recipe and the instructions for the best results.

6. Can I use the Ninja Combi for slow cooking?

Yes, the Slow Cook function is perfect for preparing stews, soups, and other dishes that require long, slow cooking. The Ninja Combi offers both high and low settings, allowing you to slow cook for up to 12 hours, giving you plenty of flexibility for meal prep or making dishes that develop rich flavours over time.

7. How do I clean the Ninja Combi after use?
After cooking, allow the unit to cool before cleaning. Remove the Combi Pan, Crisper Plate, and Bake Tray, and wash them with warm soapy water. Wipe down the inside and exterior of the appliance with a damp cloth. Never immerse the base unit in water, and always dry all parts thoroughly before storing.

8. Can I bake cakes or bread in the Ninja Combi?
Yes, the Combi Bake and Bake functions are perfect for baking cakes, bread, and other baked goods. The unit works like a traditional oven, with even heat distribution to ensure a perfectly baked result. Just be sure to follow the correct temperature and time settings for your recipe.

9. Is the Ninja Combi suitable for small kitchens?
Yes, the Ninja Combi is designed to be compact and space-efficient, making it ideal for smaller kitchens. Despite its compact size, it offers a generous capacity to cook meals for up to 6-8 people, making it perfect for family meals or batch cooking.

10. How do I troubleshoot if my Ninja Combi isn't heating properly?
If your Ninja Combi isn't heating as expected, check that the unit is plugged in and the door is securely closed. Make sure the SmartSwitch is correctly set to the desired cooking mode. If the issue persists, unplug the appliance, allow it to cool, and refer to the troubleshooting section of the user manual. If necessary, contact customer support for further assistance.

If you have any further questions, refer to the full user manual or reach out to customer support for additional help. The Ninja Combi Multicooker is designed to make cooking easier and more enjoyable, and we're here to help you get the most out of it!

CHAPTER 2: HEARTY BREAKFASTS

Baked Beans on Toast

🕐 *Prep Time: 5 minutes, Cook Time: 5 minutes, Serves: 2*

🏆 **INGREDIENTS:**
- 2 slices of bread (preferably wholemeal)
- 400 g tin of baked beans
- 50 g grated cheddar cheese (optional)
- 1 tbsp. butter
- Salt and pepper to taste

🍳 **DIRECTIONS:**
1. Place the bread slices directly on the Bake Tray.
2. Flip the SmartSwitch to AIR FRY/HOB. Select BAKE, set the temperature to 180°C, and set the time to 8 minutes. Press START/STOP to begin preheat. (The unit will preheat for 3 minutes).
3. Once preheated, slide the tray into the unit and toast the bread for 5 minutes, flipping halfway for even browning.
4. While the bread is toasting, heat the baked beans in a saucepan over medium heat on the hob. Season with salt and pepper to taste.
5. Once the toast is ready, remove it from the unit and spread with butter. Spoon the hot baked beans over the toast. Sprinkle the grated cheddar cheese on top of the beans if desired. Enjoy!

Classic Full English Breakfast

🕐 *Prep Time: 10 minutes, Cook Time: 12 minutes, Serves: 2*

🏆 **INGREDIENTS:**
- 2 sausages
- 4 rashers of back bacon
- 2 large eggs
- 2 slices of black pudding
- 2 medium tomatoes, halved
- 1 tbsp. olive oil
- Salt and pepper to taste

🍳 **DIRECTIONS:**
1. Place the Crisper Plate in the Combi Pan and set aside.
2. Close the door and flip the SmartSwitch to AIR FRY/HOB. Select AIR FRY, set the temperature to 200°C, and set the time to 17 minutes. Press START/STOP to begin preheating (The unit will preheat for 5 minutes).
3. While the unit is preheating, arrange the sausages, bacon, black pudding, and halved tomatoes onto the Crisper Plate. Drizzle with olive oil and season with salt and taste.
4. When 12 minutes remain on the timer, open the door and slide the pan into Level 1. Close the door to continue cooking.
5. When 6 minutes remain, open the door and flip the sausages, bacon, and black pudding. Close the door to continue cooking.
6. Meanwhile, fry the eggs in a saucepan until the eggs are cooked to your liking.
7. When cooking is complete, remove the pan. Serve hot with toast.

Grilled Cheese and Ham Toastie

Prep Time: 5 minutes, Cook Time: 7 minutes, Serves: 2

INGREDIENTS:
- Cooking spray
- 4 slices of bread
- 2 slices of ham
- 2 slices of cheddar cheese
- 2 tbsps. butter

DIRECTIONS:
1. Spray the Bake Tray with cooking spray.
2. Butter the outer sides of the bread slices. Arrange 1 slice of ham and 1 slice of cheddar cheese between the slices, buttered sides facing out.
3. Arrange the sandwiches on the tray and slide into Level 2.
4. Close the door and flip the SmartSwitch to AIR FRY/HOB. Select GRILL and set the time to 7 minutes. Press START/STOP to begin cooking.
5. When 4 minutes remain, open the door and flip the toastie. Close the door to continue cooking.
6. When cooking is complete, remove the tray from the unit and serve the toastie hot.

Traditional British Scones

Prep Time: 15 minutes, Cook Time: 10 minutes, Serves: 8

INGREDIENTS:
- Cooking spray
- 225 g self-raising flour
- 100 g cold butter, cubed
- 50 g caster sugar
- 1 pinch of salt
- 1 beaten egg
- 125 ml milk

DIRECTIONS:
1. Add the self-raising flour, cold butter, caster sugar, and salt in a bowl. Use your fingers to rub the butter into the flour until it resembles breadcrumbs.
2. Add the beaten egg and milk to the mixture, stirring gently until the dough comes together.
3. Roll the dough out on a lightly floured surface to about 2.5 cm thick. Use a round cutter to cut out the scones. Place scones on Bake Tray and lightly spray with cooking spray.
4. Flip the SmartSwitch to AIR FRY/HOB. Select BAKE, set the temperature to 170°C, and set the time to 13 minutes. Press START/STOP to begin preheat. (The unit will preheat for 3 minutes).
5. Once the unit has preheated, open the door and slide the tray into Level 1. Close the door to start cooking.
6. When cooking is complete, remove the tray, and serve the scones warm with clotted cream and jam.

Breakfast Porridge

Prep Time: 5 minutes, Cook Time: 4 hours on low, Serves: 4-6

INGREDIENTS:
- 200 g porridge oats
- 800 ml whole milk
- 100 ml double cream
- 50 g brown sugar
- Pinch of salt

DIRECTIONS:
1. Add the oats, milk, cream, sugar and salt in the Combi Pan and combine well. Slide the Combi Pan into Level 1.
2. Close the door and flip the SmartSwitch to AIR FRY/HOB. Select SLOW COOK, set temperature to LOW and set time to 4 hours. Press START/STOP to begin cooking.
3. When cooking is complete, stir well and serve with fruit or honey.

Avocado and Egg Toast

Prep Time: 5 minutes, Cook Time: 12 minutes, Serves: 2

INGREDIENTS:
- 2 ripe avocados
- 2 large eggs
- 2 slices of wholegrain bread
- 2 tsps. olive oil
- Salt and pepper to taste
- Red chilli flakes (optional)

DIRECTIONS:
1. Place the Crisper Plate in the Combi Pan and set aside.
2. Close the door and flip the SmartSwitch to AIR FRY/HOB.
3. Select AIR FRY, set the temperature to 180°C, and set the time to 17 minutes. Press START/STOP to begin preheating (The unit will preheat for 5 minutes).
4. Once preheated, place the bread on the Crisper Plate. Open the door and slide the pan into Level 1. Close the door to continue cooking.
5. After 3 minutes toasting, drizzle the toast with olive oil on both sides.
6. Crack the egg into a small dish, and gently crack the egg onto the toast. Close the door to continue cooking.
7. When 5 minutes remain, open the door and add the sliced avocado on top of the toast. Sprinkle with salt, pepper, and red chilli flakes if desired.
8. When cooking is complete, remove the pan and serve the avocado and egg toast hot.

Slow Cooked Breakfast Casserole

🕐 Prep Time: 15 minutes, Cook Time: 4 hours on low, Serves: 6

🏆 INGREDIENTS:
- 6 eggs, beaten
- 500 g diced potatoes
- 200 g cooked sausage, sliced
- 1 onion, chopped
- 200 ml milk
- 100 g grated cheddar cheese
- Salt and pepper to taste

🍳 DIRECTIONS:
1. Mix the potatoes, sausage, and onion in the Combi Pan.
2. Whisk the eggs, milk, and cheese together, season with salt and pepper, and pour over the potato mixture.
3. Slide the Combi Pan into Level 1. Close the door and flip the SmartSwitch to AIR FRY/HOB. Select SLOW COOK, set temperature to LOW and set time to 4 hours. Press START/STOP to begin cooking, until the eggs are fully set.
4. When cooking is complete, cut into portions and serve hot.

Toad in the Hole

🕐 Prep Time: 10 minutes, Cook Time: 25 minutes, Serves: 4

🏆 INGREDIENTS:
- 4 sausages
- 200 g plain flour
- 2 large eggs
- 300 ml milk
- 1 tbsp. vegetable oil
- Salt and pepper to taste

🍳 DIRECTIONS:
1. Add sausages to the Combi Pan and drizzle with vegetable oil. Set aside.
2. Flip the SmartSwitch to AIR FRY/HOB. Select BAKE, set temperature to 200°C, and set time to 28 minutes. Press START/STOP to begin preheat. (The unit will preheat for 3 minutes).
3. When preheat is complete, open door and slide pan into Level 1. Close door to start cooking.
4. Meanwhile, whisk together the flour, eggs, milk, salt, and pepper in a bowl to form the batter.
5. When 15 minutes remain, pour the batter over the sausages and close the door to continue cooking.
6. When cooking is complete, pull the Combi Pan out. Let the Toad in the Hole cool for a few minutes before serving with gravy.

Grilled Bacon and Tomato Sandwich

🕐 *Prep Time: 5 minutes, Cook Time: 6 minutes, Serves: 2*

🍳 **INGREDIENTS:**
- Cooking spray
- 4 slices of bread
- 4 rashers of bacon
- 1 tomato, sliced
- 2 slices of cheddar cheese
- 2 tsps. butter

🍳 **DIRECTIONS:**
1. Spray the Bake Tray with cooking spray.
2. Spread 1 tsp. butter on one side of each slice of bread. Arrange 2 bread slices on the tray, buttered side down, and top each with a slice of cheddar cheese. Add the tomato slices and bacon on top of the bread. Top with the remaining bread. Slide the tray into Level 2.
3. Close the door and flip the SmartSwitch to AIR FRY/HOB. Select GRILL and set the time to 6 minutes. Press START/STOP to begin cooking.
4. When 3 minutes remain, open the door and flip the sandwiches. Close the door to continue cooking.
5. When cooking is complete, remove the tray from the unit and serve the sandwich hot.

Rice Pudding

🕐 *Prep Time: 5 minutes, Cook Time: 4 hours on low, Serves: 4-6*

🍳 **INGREDIENTS:**
- 100 g pudding rice
- 750 ml whole milk
- 50 g caster sugar
- 1 tsp. vanilla extract
- 1 knob of butter

🍳 **DIRECTIONS:**
1. Mix all the ingredients in the Combi Pan and combine well. Slide the Combi Pan into Level 1.
2. Close the door and flip the SmartSwitch to AIR FRY/HOB. Select SLOW COOK, set temperature to LOW and set time to 4 hours. Press START/STOP to begin cooking.
3. When cooking is complete, stir well and serve warm.

Sausage and Mushroom Breakfast Casserole

🕐 *Prep Time: 10 minutes, Cook Time: 30 minutes, Serves: 4*

🏆 **INGREDIENTS:**
- 4 sausages (approx. 250 g)
- 100 g button mushrooms, sliced
- 4 large eggs
- 200 ml milk
- 1 tsp. mustard powder
- 100 g grated cheddar cheese
- 1 tbsp. olive oil
- Salt and pepper to taste

🍳 **DIRECTIONS:**
1. Add the sausages in a pan, drizzle with olive oil, and saute for about 10 minutes until browned. Slice the sausages into pieces.
2. Then add the sliced sausages, mushrooms to the Combi Pan.
3. In a separate bowl, whisk together the eggs, milk, mustard powder, and grated cheese. Season with salt and pepper.
4. Pour the egg mixture over the sausages and mushrooms in the pan.
5. Flip the SmartSwitch to AIR FRY/HOB. Select BAKE, set the temperature to 180°C, and set the time to 23 minutes. Press START/STOP to begin preheat. (The unit will preheat for 3 minutes).
6. When preheat is complete, open door and slide pan into Level 1. Close door to start cooking, until the egg is set and golden brown.
7. When cooking is complete, remove the pan, let it cool slightly, slice, and serve hot.

Vegetarian Breakfast Hash

🕐 *Prep Time: 10 minutes, Cook Time: 20 minutes, Serves: 4-6*

🏆 **INGREDIENTS:**
- 2 large potatoes, peeled and diced
- 1 red pepper, diced
- 1 yellow pepper, diced
- 1 small onion, chopped
- 100 g mushrooms, sliced
- 1 tbsp. olive oil
- Salt and pepper to taste

🍳 **DIRECTIONS:**
1. Place the Crisper Plate in the Combi Pan and set aside.
2. Close the door and flip the SmartSwitch to AIR FRY/HOB. Select AIR FRY, set the temperature to 200°C, and set the time to 25 minutes. Press START/STOP to begin preheating (The unit will preheat for 5 minutes).
3. While the unit is preheating, toss the diced potatoes, peppers, onion, and mushrooms with olive oil, salt, and pepper in a bowl.
4. When preheated, place the hash mixture onto the Crisper Plate. Open the door and slide the pan into Level 1. Close the door to continue cooking.
5. When 10 minutes remain on the timer, open the door and toss the vegetables. Close the door to continue cooking.
6. When cooking is complete, remove the pan and serve hot.

Beef Steak and Spinach Pasta

🕐 *Prep: 10 minutes, Total Cook Time: 24 minutes, Steam: approx. 10 minutes, Cook: 14 minutes, Serves: 4*

🍸 INGREDIENTS:

LEVEL 1 (Combi Pan):
- 300 g fusilli pasta
- 700 ml beef stock
- 2 tbsps. tomato purée
- 1 tsp. garlic powder
- ½ tsp. dried basil
- Salt and black pepper to taste

LEVEL 2 (Bake Tray):
- 4 sirloin steaks
- 100 g fresh spinach, chopped
- 1 tbsp. olive oil
- 1 tsp. dried rosemary
- Salt and black pepper to taste

🍴 DIRECTIONS:

1. Place the fusilli pasta, beef stock, tomato purée, garlic powder, basil, salt, and black pepper into the Combi Pan and stir to combine. Slide the pan into Level 1.
2. Toss the sirloin steaks with olive oil, rosemary, salt, and black pepper. Arrange the beef steaks on the Bake Tray and slide the tray into Level 2.
3. Close the door and flip the SmartSwitch to COMBI COOKER. Select COMBI MEALS, set temperature to 175°C, and set the time to 14 minutes. Press START/STOP to begin cooking (The unit will steam for approx. 10 minutes).
4. When 5 minutes remain, open the door and add the spinach to the pan. Close the door to continue cooking.
5. When cooking is complete, remove the tray and pan. Rest the sirloin steaks for a few minutes, then slice and stir them into the pasta with spinach. Serve hot.

Salmon and Leek with Quinoa

🕐 *Prep: 10 minutes, Total Cook Time: 20 minutes, Steam: approx. 6 minutes, Cook: 14 minutes, Serves: 4*

🍸 INGREDIENTS:

LEVEL 1 (Combi Pan):
- 300 g quinoa
- 700 ml fish stock
- 1 small leek, sliced
- 1 tbsp. olive oil
- Salt and black pepper to taste

LEVEL 2 (Bake Tray):
- 4 salmon fillets
- 1 tbsp. lemon juice
- 1 tsp. dried dill
- Salt and black pepper to taste

🍴 DIRECTIONS:

1. Place the quinoa, fish stock, sliced leek, olive oil, salt, and black pepper into the Combi Pan and stir to combine. Slide the pan into Level 1.
2. Drizzle the salmon fillets with lemon juice and sprinkle with dill, salt, and black pepper. Place the fillets on the Bake Tray and slide the tray into Level 2.
3. Close the door and flip the SmartSwitch to COMBI COOKER. Select COMBI MEALS, set temperature to 175°C, and set time to 14 minutes. Press START/STOP to begin cooking (The unit will steam for approx. 6 minutes).
4. When cooking is complete, remove the tray and pan. Stir the salmon and quinoa together and serve hot.

Chicken Alfredo Pasta

Prep: 10 minutes, Total Cook Time: 25 minutes, Steam: approx. 10 minutes, Cook: 15 minutes, Serves: 4

INGREDIENTS:

LEVEL 1 (Combi Pan):
- 300 g tagliatelle pasta
- 600 ml chicken stock
- 100 ml double cream
- 100 g mushrooms, sliced
- 1 tbsp. butter
- 1 tsp. garlic powder
- ½ tsp. dried basil
- Salt and black pepper to taste

LEVEL 2 (Bake Tray):
- 2 chicken breasts, sliced
- 1 tbsp. olive oil
- 1 tsp. dried oregano
- ½ tsp. ground black pepper
- Salt to taste

DIRECTIONS:

1. Place the tagliatelle pasta, mushrooms, chicken stock, double cream, butter, garlic powder, basil, salt, and black pepper into the Combi Pan and stir to combine. Slide the pan into Level 1.
2. Toss the chicken breast slices with olive oil, oregano, ground black pepper, and salt. Arrange the chicken on the Bake Tray and slide the tray into Level 2.
3. Close the door and flip the SmartSwitch to COMBI COOKER. Select COMBI MEALS, set temperature to 200°C, and set the time to 15 minutes. Press START/STOP to begin cooking (The unit will steam for approx. 10 minutes).
4. When cooking is complete, remove the tray and pan. Stir the cooked chicken into the creamy pasta and serve.

Lamb Kofta and Couscous

Prep: 15 minutes, Total Cook Time: 20 minutes, Steam: approx. 8 minutes, Cook: 12 minutes, Serves: 4

INGREDIENTS:

LEVEL 1 (Combi Pan):
- 300 g couscous
- 500 ml vegetable stock
- 1 tsp. ground cumin
- 1 tsp. paprika
- Salt and black pepper to taste

LEVEL 2 (Bake Tray):
- 400 g lamb mince
- 1 small onion, grated
- 2 cloves garlic, minced
- 1 tbsp. ground coriander
- 1 tsp. dried mint
- Salt and black pepper to taste

DIRECTIONS:

1. Place the couscous, vegetable stock, cumin, paprika, salt, and black pepper into the Combi Pan and stir to combine. Slide the pan into Level 1.
2. In a large bowl, combine the lamb mince, grated onion, garlic, coriander, mint, salt, and pepper. Roll the mixture into kofta-shaped patties and place on the Bake Tray. Slide the tray into Level 2.
3. Close the door and flip the SmartSwitch to COMBI COOKER. Select COMBI MEALS, set temperature to 190°C, and set time to 12 minutes. Press START/STOP to begin cooking (The unit will steam for approx. 8 minutes).
4. When cooking is complete, remove the tray and pan. Serve the lamb kofta on a bed of couscous.

Beef and Broccoli Meal

🕐 *Prep: 10 minutes, Total Cook Time: 22 minutes, Steam: approx. 8 minutes, Cook: 14 minutes, Serves: 4*

🏆 **INGREDIENTS:**

LEVEL 1 (Combi Pan):
- 200 g basmati rice
- 500 ml beef stock
- 1 tbsp. soy sauce
- 1 tsp. ground ginger
- Salt and black pepper to taste

LEVEL 2 (Bake Tray):
- 400 g beef strips
- 1 tbsp. olive oil
- 1 tbsp. soy sauce
- 1 tsp. sesame oil
- 120 g broccoli florets
- 1 spring onion, chopped

🍳 **DIRECTIONS:**

1. Place the basmati rice, beef stock, soy sauce, ginger, salt, and black pepper into the Combi Pan and stir to combine. Slide the pan into Level 1.
2. In a bowl, toss the beef strips, and broccoli with olive oil, soy sauce, sesame oil, salt, and black pepper. Arrange the beef and broccoli on the Bake Tray and slide the tray into Level 2.
3. Close the door and flip the SmartSwitch to COMBI COOKER. Select COMBI MEALS, set temperature to 175°C, and set time to 14 minutes. Press START/STOP to begin cooking (The unit will steam for approx. 8 minutes).
4. When cooking is complete, remove the tray and pan. Stir the beef and broccoli into the rice and serve garnished with spring onions.

Spaghetti Bolognese

🕐 *Prep Time: 15 minutes, Cook Time: 25 minutes, Serves: 4*

🏆 **INGREDIENTS:**
- 400 g spaghetti
- 400 g chopped tomatoes
- 400 g minced beef
- 1 onion, chopped
- 2 cloves garlic, minced
- 1 carrot, diced
- 2 tbsps. tomato purée
- 1 tsp. dried oregano
- Salt and pepper to taste

🍳 **DIRECTIONS:**

1. Add the spaghetti and 1 L of water to the Combi Pan.
2. Insert the Combi Pan into Level 1. Close the door and flip the SmartSwitch to COMBI COOKER. Select RICE/PASTA and set to PASTA. Press START/STOP to begin cooking (The unit will display an animation while cooking; program will take approx. 15 minutes to complete).
3. While the spaghetti cooks, heat a separate pan and sauté the onion and garlic over medium-high heat. Add minced beef and cook until browned. Stir in chopped tomatoes, tomato purée, carrot, oregano, salt, and pepper. Simmer for 10 minutes.
4. When cooking is complete, the unit will beep. Stir the Bolognese sauce to combine with the cooked spaghetti and serve warm.

Mussels and Garlic Pasta

Prep Time: 10 minutes, Cook Time: 20 minutes, Serves: 4

INGREDIENTS:
- 450 g spaghetti
- 500 g mussels, cleaned
- 3 cloves garlic, minced
- 1 tbsp. olive oil
- 1 L fish stock
- 1 tbsp. butter
- Fresh parsley, chopped, for garnish
- Salt and pepper to taste

DIRECTIONS:
1. Add the spaghetti, mussels, garlic, olive oil, fish stock, salt, and pepper into the Combi Pan. Insert the Combi Pan into Level 1.
2. Close the door and flip the SmartSwitch to COMBI COOKER. Select RICE/PASTA and set to PASTA. Press START/STOP to begin cooking (The unit will display an animation while cooking; program will take approx. 20 minutes to complete).
3. When cooking is complete, the unit will beep. Remove the mussels that haven't opened. Stir in the butter for a creamy finish. Taste and adjust seasoning if necessary.
4. Serve warm, garnished with fresh parsley.

Chicken and Pesto Pasta

Prep: 10 minutes, Total Cook Time: 25 minutes, Steam: approx. 10 minutes, Cook: 15 minutes, Serves: 4

INGREDIENTS:

LEVEL 1 (Combi Pan):
- 300 g penne pasta
- 700 ml vegetable stock
- 1 tbsp. olive oil
- 2 tbsps. pesto sauce
- ½ tsp. garlic powder
- Salt and black pepper to taste

LEVEL 2 (Bake Tray):
- 4 chicken drumsticks
- 1 tbsp. olive oil
- 1 tsp. dried oregano
- 1 tsp. dried thyme
- Salt and pepper to taste

DIRECTIONS:
1. Place the penne pasta, vegetable stock, olive oil, pesto sauce, garlic powder, salt, and black pepper into the Combi Pan and stir to combine. Slide the pan into Level 1.
2. Toss the chicken drumsticks with olive oil, oregano, thyme, salt, and black pepper in a bowl. Arrange the chicken drumsticks on the Bake Tray and slide the tray into Level 2.
3. Close the door and flip the SmartSwitch to COMBI COOKER. Select COMBI MEALS, set temperature to 200°C, and set the time to 15 minutes. Press START/STOP to begin cooking (The unit will steam for approx. 10 minutes).
4. When cooking is complete, remove the tray and pan. Serve the chicken drumsticks with the pesto pasta.

Thai Red Curry with Tofu and Rice

🕐 *Prep: 15 minutes, Total Cook Time: 20 minutes, Steam: approx. 8 minutes, Cook: 12 minutes, Serves: 4*

🍸 INGREDIENTS:
LEVEL 1 (Combi Pan):
- 200 g jasmine rice
- 500 ml coconut milk
- 2 tbsps. red curry paste
- 1 tbsp. soy sauce
- Salt to taste

LEVEL 2 (Bake Tray):
- 400 g firm tofu, cubed

- 1 red pepper, chopped
- 1 yellow pepper, chopped
- 1 small onion, chopped
- 60 g green beans, trimmed
- 1 tsp. garlic powder
- 1 tsp. paprika
- 1 tbsp. olive oil
- Salt and pepper

🍳 DIRECTIONS:
1. Place the jasmine rice, coconut milk, red curry paste, soy sauce, and salt into the Combi Pan and stir to combine. Slide the pan into Level 1.
2. In a large bowl, toss the tofu, red pepper, yellow pepper, onion, green beans, garlic powder, paprika, olive oil, salt, and pepper. Arrange the mixture on the Bake Tray and slide the tray into Level 2.
3. Close the door and flip the SmartSwitch to COMBI COOKER. Select COMBI MEALS, set temperature to 175°C, and set time to 12 minutes. Press START/STOP to begin cooking (The unit will steam for approx. 8 minutes).
4. When cooking is complete, remove the tray and pan. Stir the tofu and vegetables into the rice and serve hot.

Pork Chop and Pumpkin Linguine

🕐 *Prep: 10 minutes, Total Cook Time: 22 minutes, Steam: approx. 10 minutes, Cook: 12 minutes, Serves: 4*

🍸 INGREDIENTS:
LEVEL 1 (Combi Pan):
- 300 g linguine
- 700 ml vegetable stock
- 100 g pumpkin, cubed
- 1 tbsp. olive oil
- 1 tsp. dried sage
- ½ tsp. garlic powder

- Salt and black pepper to taste

LEVEL 2 (Bake Tray):
- 4 pork chops
- 1 tbsp. olive oil
- 1 tsp. ground black pepper
- 1 tsp. dried thyme
- Salt to taste

🍳 DIRECTIONS:
1. Place the linguine, pumpkin, vegetable stock, olive oil, sage, garlic powder, salt, and black pepper into the Combi Pan and stir to combine. Slide the pan into Level 1.
2. Rub the pork chops with olive oil, ground black pepper, thyme, and salt. Arrange the pork chops on the Bake Tray and slide the tray into Level 2.
3. Close the door and flip the SmartSwitch to COMBI COOKER. Select COMBI MEALS, set temperature to 190°C, and set the time to 12 minutes. Press START/STOP to begin cooking (The unit will steam for approx. 10 minutes).
4. When cooking is complete, remove the tray and pan. Rest the pork chops for a few minutes, then slice and stir them into the pasta. Serve hot.

Pea and Ham Rice Pilaf

🕐 *Prep Time: 10 minutes, Cook Time: 20 minutes, Serves: 4*

🏆 **INGREDIENTS:**
- 300 g basmati rice
- 150 g cooked ham, diced
- 100 g frozen peas
- 750 ml chicken stock
- 1 onion, chopped
- 1 tbsp. olive oil
- 1 tsp. dried thyme
- Salt and pepper to taste
- Fresh parsley, chopped (optional)

🍴 **DIRECTIONS:**
1. Add the basmati rice, chicken stock, thyme, diced ham, frozen peas, onion, olive oil, salt, and pepper into the Combi Pan. Insert the Combi Pan into Level 1.
2. Close the door and flip the SmartSwitch to COMBI COOKER. Select RICE and press START/STOP to begin cooking (The unit will display an animation while cooking; program will take approx. 20 minutes to complete).
3. When cooking is complete, the unit will beep. Stir the mixture to combine and keep warm until ready to serve.
4. Garnish with fresh parsley (optional) and serve.

Creamy Tomato and Basil Rice

🕐 *Prep Time: 15 minutes, Cook Time: 25 minutes, Serves: 4*

🏆 **INGREDIENTS:**
- 300 g long-grain rice
- 400 g tin chopped tomatoes
- 750 ml vegetable stock
- 2 tbsps. tomato purée
- 1 onion, chopped
- 1 garlic clove, minced
- 150 ml double cream
- 1 tbsp. olive oil
- Fresh basil leaves, chopped
- Salt and pepper to taste

🍴 **DIRECTIONS:**
1. Add the rice, chopped tomatoes, vegetable stock, tomato purée, double cream, olive oil, onion and garlic into the Combi Pan. Insert the Combi Pan into Level 1.
1. Close the door and flip the SmartSwitch to COMBI COOKER. Select RICE and press START/STOP to begin cooking (The unit will display an animation while cooking; program will take approx. 25 minutes to complete).
2. When cooking is complete, the unit will beep.
3. Stir in chopped basil and mix well. Season with salt and pepper. Serve warm.

CHAPTER 4: DINNER PLEASURES

Salmon and Spinach Risotto

🕐 *Prep: 10 minutes, Total Cook Time: 20 minutes, Steam: approx. 6 minutes, Cook: 14 minutes, Serves: 4*

INGREDIENTS:

LEVEL 1 (Combi Pan):
- 300 g basmati rice
- 800 ml fish stock
- 100 g fresh spinach
- 1 tsp. dill
- ½ tsp. ground black pepper
- 1 tsp. garlic powder
- ½ tsp. salt

LEVEL 2 (Bake Tray):
- 4 salmon fillets
- 1 tbsp. olive oil
- 1 tsp. lemon zest
- 1 tsp. mustard seeds
- Salt and black pepper to taste

DIRECTIONS:

1. Place the rice, fish stock, dill, black pepper, garlic powder, salt, and spinach into the Combi Pan and stir to combine well. Slide the pan into Level 1.
2. Toss the salmon fillets with olive oil, lemon zest, mustard seeds, salt, and black pepper. Arrange the salmon fillets on the Bake Tray and slide the tray into Level 2.
3. Close the door and flip the SmartSwitch to COMBI COOKER. Select COMBI MEALS, set temperature to 175°C, and set the time to 14 minutes. Press START/STOP to begin cooking (The unit will steam for approx. 6 minutes).
4. When cooking is complete, remove the tray and pan. Serve the salmon on top of the rice mixture.

Creamy Seafood Pasta

🕐 *Prep Time: 10 minutes, Cook Time: 20 minutes, Serves: 4*

INGREDIENTS:
- 400 g linguine pasta
- 200 g mixed seafood (prawns, mussels, squid)
- 200 ml double cream
- 900 ml water
- 1 clove garlic, minced
- 1 tbsp. olive oil
- 1 tbsp. white wine (optional)
- 1 tsp. lemon zest
- Salt and pepper to taste
- Fresh parsley, chopped, for garnish

DIRECTIONS:

1. Add the linguine pasta, mixed seafood, water, garlic, olive oil, white wine (if using), salt, and pepper into the Combi Pan. Insert the Combi Pan into Level 1.
2. Close the door and flip the SmartSwitch to COMBI COOKER. Select RICE/PASTA and set to PASTA. Press START/STOP to begin cooking (The unit will display an animation while cooking; program will take approx. 20 minutes to complete).
3. When cooking is complete, the unit will beep. Stir in the double cream and lemon zest, mixing well.
4. Taste and adjust seasoning if necessary. Serve warm, garnished with fresh parsley.

Beef and Mushroom Stroganoff with Egg Noodles

🕐 *Prep: 15 minutes, Total Cook Time: 24 minutes, Steam: approx. 10 minutes, Cook: 14 minutes, Serves: 4*

🏆 **INGREDIENTS:**

LEVEL 1 (Combi Pan):
- 300 g egg noodles
- 700 ml beef stock
- 1 tbsp. Dijon mustard
- 1 tsp. dried thyme
- Salt and black pepper to taste

LEVEL 2 (Bake Tray):
- 2 beef steaks, sliced thinly
- 200 g mushrooms, sliced
- 2 tbsps. olive oil
- 1 small onion, chopped
- 1 clove garlic, minced
- 1 tbsp. flour
- 100 ml double cream

🍳 **DIRECTIONS:**

1. Place the egg noodles, beef stock, Dijon mustard, thyme, salt, and black pepper into the Combi Pan and stir to combine. Slide the pan into Level 1.
2. In a large bowl, toss the beef slices with olive oil, onion, garlic, and salt and pepper. Transfer the beef mixture to the Bake Tray and slide the tray into Level 2.
3. Close the door and flip the SmartSwitch to COMBI COOKER. Select COMBI MEALS, set temperature to 180°C, and set time to 14 minutes. Press START/STOP to begin cooking (The unit will steam for approx. 10 minutes).
4. When 7 minutes remain, open the door and add the mushrooms and flour to the beef mixture. Close the door to continue cooking.
5. When cooking is complete, remove the tray and pan. Stir in the double cream into the beef stroganoff and serve with the egg noodles.

Vegetable Mac and Cheese

🕐 *Prep Time: 10 minutes, Cook Time: 20 minutes, Serves: 4*

🏆 **INGREDIENTS:**
- 400 g macaroni pasta, cooked
- 200 g broccoli florets
- 200 g cheddar cheese, grated
- 200 ml milk
- 700 ml water
- 1 tbsp. butter
- 1 tbsp. plain flour
- Salt and pepper to taste

🍳 **DIRECTIONS:**

1. Add the macaroni, broccoli florets, milk, water, salt, and pepper into the Combi Pan. Insert the Combi Pan into Level 1.
2. Close the door and flip the SmartSwitch to COMBI COOKER. Select RICE/PASTA and set to PASTA. Press START/STOP to begin cooking (The unit will display an animation while cooking; program will take approx. 20 minutes to complete).
3. While the macaroni cooks, heat a separate pan and add the butter and flour to make a roux, then stir in the grated cheese, until the cheese sauce has thickened. Set aside.
4. When cooking is complete, the unit will beep. Stir the cheese mixture to combine with the macaroni. Serve warm.

Sweet and Sour Pork with Rice

🕐 Prep: 10 minutes, Total Cook Time: 23 minutes, Steam: approx. 10 minutes, Cook: 13 minutes, Serves: 4

🍴 **INGREDIENTS:**

LEVEL 1 (Combi Pan):
- 300 g long-grain white rice
- 750 ml chicken stock
- 1 tbsp. rice vinegar
- 1 tbsp. soy sauce
- Salt and black pepper to taste

LEVEL 2 (Bake Tray):
- 400 g pork tenderloin, cut into strips
- 70 g pineapple chunks (fresh or canned)
- ½ red pepper, sliced
- ½ green pepper, sliced
- 1 tbsp. olive oil
- 60 ml sweet and sour sauce

👨‍🍳 **DIRECTIONS:**

1. Place the long-grain white rice, chicken stock, rice vinegar, soy sauce, salt, and black pepper into the Combi Pan and stir to combine. Slide the pan into Level 1.
2. In a large bowl, toss the pork strips, pineapple chunks, red pepper, green pepper and olive oil. Arrange the mixture on the Bake Tray, drizzle with sweet and sour sauce and slide the tray into Level 2.
3. Close the door and flip the SmartSwitch to COMBI COOKER. Select COMBI MEALS, set temperature to 190°C, and set time to 13 minutes. Press START/STOP to begin cooking (The unit will steam for approx. 10 minutes).
4. When cooking is complete, remove the tray and pan. Stir the pork and vegetables into the rice and serve.

Prawn and Tomato Pasta

🕐 Prep: 10 minutes, Total Cook Time: 20 minutes, Steam: approx. 8 minutes, Cook: 12 minutes, Serves: 4

🍴 **INGREDIENTS:**

LEVEL 1 (Combi Pan):
- 300 g spaghetti
- 700 ml fish stock
- 100 g asparagus, chopped
- 1 tbsp. tomato purée
- 1 tsp. dried oregano
- ½ tsp. chilli flakes
- Salt and black pepper to taste

LEVEL 2 (Bake Tray):
- 300 g prawns, peeled and deveined
- 1 tbsp. olive oil
- 2 cloves garlic, minced
- 1 tbsp. lemon juice
- ½ tsp. smoked paprika
- Salt and black pepper to taste

👨‍🍳 **DIRECTIONS:**

1. Place the spaghetti, asparagus, fish stock, tomato purée, oregano, chilli flakes, salt, and black pepper into the Combi Pan and stir to combine. Slide the pan into Level 1.
2. Toss the prawns with olive oil, garlic, lemon juice, smoked paprika, salt, and black pepper. Arrange the prawns on the Bake Tray and slide the tray into Level 2.
3. Close the door and flip the SmartSwitch to COMBI COOKER. Select COMBI MEALS, set temperature to 175°C, and set the time to 12 minutes. Press START/STOP to begin cooking (The unit will steam for approx. 8 minutes).
4. When cooking is complete, remove the tray and pan. Stir the prawns into the pasta and serve immediately.

Lemon and Herb Rice Pilaf

🕐 *Prep Time: 10 minutes, Cook Time: 20 minutes, Serves: 3-4*

🍽 INGREDIENTS:
- 300 g basmati rice
- 1 lemon, zested and juiced
- 750 ml vegetable stock
- 1 onion, chopped
- 1 garlic clove, minced
- 30 g butter
- 1 tbsp. olive oil
- 1 tsp. dried mixed herbs
- Salt and pepper to taste
- Fresh parsley, chopped (optional)

🍳 DIRECTIONS:
1. Add the basmati rice, vegetable stock, lemon juice, lemon zest, onion and garlic into the Combi Pan. Stir in the mixed herbs, olive oil, butter, and cooked rice. Season with salt and pepper. Insert the Combi Pan into Level 1.
2. Close the door and flip the SmartSwitch to COMBI COOKER. Select RICE and press START/STOP to begin cooking (The unit will display an animation while cooking; program will take approx. 20 minutes to complete).
3. When cooking is complete, the unit will beep.
4. Garnish with fresh parsley (optional) and serve warm.

Meatball and Peppers Pasta

🕐 *Prep: 15 minutes, Total Cook Time: 22 minutes, Steam: approx. 10 minutes, Cook: 12 minutes, Serves: 4*

🍽 INGREDIENTS:

LEVEL 1 (Combi Pan):
- 300 g spaghetti
- 800 ml tomato passata
- 1 tbsp. olive oil
- 1 tsp. garlic powder
- ½ tsp. dried oregano
- Salt and black pepper to taste

LEVEL 2 (Bake Tray):
- 500 g beef meatballs
- 1 red pepper, sliced
- 1 tbsp. olive oil
- ½ tsp. smoked paprika
- Salt and black pepper to taste

🍳 DIRECTIONS:
1. Place the spaghetti, tomato passata, olive oil, garlic powder, oregano, salt, and black pepper into the Combi Pan and stir to combine. Slide the pan into Level 1.
2. Toss the meatballs with the sliced peppers, olive oil, smoked paprika, salt, and black pepper in a bowl. Arrange the meatball and pepper mixture on the Bake Tray and slide the tray into Level 2.
3. Close the door and flip the SmartSwitch to COMBI COOKER. Select COMBI MEALS, set temperature to 180°C, and set the time to 12 minutes. Press START/STOP to begin cooking (The unit will steam for approx. 10 minutes).
4. When cooking is complete, remove the tray and pan. Stir the meatballs and peppers into the pasta and serve hot.

Chicken and Pea Risotto

Prep: 10 minutes, Total Cook Time: 26 minutes, Steam: approx. 10 minutes, Cook: 16 minutes, Serves: 4

INGREDIENTS:

LEVEL 1 (Combi Pan):
- 300 g Arborio rice
- 800 ml chicken stock
- 100 g frozen peas
- 1 tsp. dried thyme
- Salt and black pepper to taste

LEVEL 2 (Bake Tray):
- 4 chicken thighs
- 1 tbsp. olive oil
- 1 tsp. garlic powder
- Salt and black pepper to taste

DIRECTIONS:

1. Place the Arborio rice, chicken stock, peas, thyme, salt, and black pepper into the Combi Pan and stir to combine. Slide the pan into Level 1.
2. Rub the chicken thighs with olive oil, garlic powder, salt, and black pepper. Arrange the chicken thighs on the Bake Tray and slide the tray into Level 2.
3. Close the door and flip the SmartSwitch to COMBI COOKER. Select COMBI MEALS, set temperature to 200°C, and set time to 16 minutes. Press START/STOP to begin cooking (The unit will steam for approx. 10 minutes).
4. When cooking is complete, remove the tray and pan. Serve the chicken thighs alongside the creamy risotto.

Spicy Chilli Rice

Prep Time: 10 minutes, Cook Time: 25 minutes, Serves: 4

INGREDIENTS:
- 300 g jasmine rice
- 400 g tin kidney beans, drained
- 750 ml chicken stock
- 1 onion, chopped
- 1 garlic clove, minced
- 1 red chilli, chopped
- 1 tsp. ground cumin
- 1 tsp. ground paprika
- 1 tbsp. tomato purée
- 1 tbsp. olive oil
- Salt and pepper to taste

DIRECTIONS:

1. Add the jasmine rice, drained kidney beans, onion, garlic, red chilli, chicken stock, olive oil, tomato purée, ground cumin, and paprika into the Combi Pan and combine well. Insert the Combi Pan into Level 1.
3. Close the door and flip the SmartSwitch to COMBI COOKER. Select RICE and press START/STOP to begin cooking (The unit will display an animation while cooking; program will take approx. 25 minutes to complete).
2. When cooking is complete, the unit will beep.
3. Season with salt and pepper to taste. Serve warm.

Grilled Lamb Steak with Basil Pasta

🕐 *Prep: 15 minutes, Total Cook Time: 24 minutes, Steam: approx. 10 minutes, Cook: 14 minutes, Serves: 4*

🏆 **INGREDIENTS:**

LEVEL 1 (Combi Pan):
- 300 g farfalle pasta
- 800 ml lamb stock
- 100 g sweet potatoes, cubed
- 2 tbsps. olive oil
- 1 tsp. dried basil
- 1 tsp. ground coriander

- Salt and black pepper to taste

LEVEL 2 (Bake Tray):
- 4 lamb steaks
- 1 tbsp. olive oil
- 1 tsp. garlic powder
- 1 tsp. dried oregano
- Salt and black pepper to taste

🍳 **DIRECTIONS:**

1 Place the farfalle pasta, sweet potatoes, lamb stock, olive oil, dried basil, ground coriander, salt, and black pepper into the Combi Pan and stir to combine. Slide the pan into Level 1.

2 Rub the lamb steaks with olive oil, garlic powder, oregano, salt, and black pepper. Arrange the lamb steaks on the Bake Tray and slide the tray into Level 2.

3 Close the door and flip the SmartSwitch to COMBI COOKER. Select COMBI MEALS, set temperature to 190°C, and set the time to 14 minutes. Press START/STOP to begin cooking (The unit will steam for approx. 10 minutes).

4 When cooking is complete, remove the tray and pan. Rest the lamb steaks for a few minutes, then slice and serve with the pasta.

Mediterranean Chicken with Couscous

🕐 *Prep: 15 minutes, Total Cook Time: 26 minutes, Steam: approx. 10 minutes, Cook: 16 minutes, Serves: 4*

🏆 **INGREDIENTS:**

LEVEL 1 (Combi Pan):
- 250 g couscous
- 500 ml chicken stock
- 1 tbsp. olive oil
- 1 tsp. dried oregano
- Salt and black pepper to taste

LEVEL 2 (Bake Tray):
- 4 chicken breasts
- 1 tsp. paprika
- 1 tsp. ground cumin
- 1 tbsp. lemon juice
- 1 tbsp. olive oil
- 60 g cherry tomatoes, halved
- 25 g black olives, sliced

🍳 **DIRECTIONS:**

1 Place the couscous, chicken stock, olive oil, oregano, salt, and black pepper into the Combi Pan and stir to combine. Slide the pan into Level 1.

2 Rub the chicken breasts with paprika, cumin, lemon juice, olive oil, salt, and black pepper. Arrange the chicken breasts on the Bake Tray. Scatter the cherry tomatoes and black olives around the chicken. And slide the tray into Level 2.

3 Close the door and flip the SmartSwitch to COMBI COOKER. Select COMBI MEALS, set temperature to 200°C, and set time to 16 minutes. Press START/STOP to begin cooking (The unit will steam for approx. 10 minutes).

4 When cooking is complete, remove the tray and pan. Fluff the couscous and serve with the chicken and vegetables.

Stuffed Chicken Breast with Spinach and Feta

Prep: 20 minutes, Total Cook Time: 30 minutes, Steam: approx. 8 minutes, Cook: 22 minutes, Serves: 4

INGREDIENTS:

- 4 chicken breasts
- 150 g spinach, wilted
- 100 g feta cheese, crumbled
- 1 tbsp. olive oil
- Salt and pepper, to taste
- 120 ml water, for steaming

DIRECTIONS:

1. Pour 120 ml of water in the Combi Pan for steaming and place the Crisper Plate on top.
2. In a bowl, combine wilted spinach, crumbled feta cheese, salt, and pepper.
3. Cut a pocket in each chicken breast and stuff with the spinach and feta mixture.
4. Drizzle olive oil over the chicken breasts and season with salt and pepper.
5. Arrange the stuffed chicken breasts on the Crisper Plate. Slide the pan into Level 1.
6. Close the door and flip the SmartSwitch to COMBI COOKER. Select COMBI CRISP, set temperature to 205°C and set time to 22 minutes. Press START/STOP to begin cooking (The unit will steam for 8 minutes before crisping).
7. After 10 minutes, open the door and flip the chicken breasts. Close the door to continue cooking.
8. When cooking is complete, remove the pan from the unit, slice, and serve with roast potatoes or a salad.

Herb-Crusted Leg of Lamb

Prep: 15 minutes, Total Cook Time: 50 minutes, Steam: approx. 10 minutes, Cook: 40 minutes, Serves: 4-6

INGREDIENTS:

- 1.2 kg leg of lamb
- 3 cloves garlic, minced
- 2 tbsps. fresh rosemary, chopped
- 2 tbsps. olive oil
- Salt and pepper, to taste
- 240 ml water, for steaming

DIRECTIONS:

1. Pour 240 ml of water in the Combi Pan for steaming and place the Crisper Plate on top.
2. In a small bowl, combine minced garlic, rosemary, olive oil, salt, and pepper. Rub the herb mixture all over the lamb leg.
3. Arrange the seasoned lamb leg on the Crisper Plate. Slide the pan into Level 1.
4. Close the door and flip the SmartSwitch to COMBI COOKER. Select COMBI CRISP, set temperature to 200°C and set time to 40 minutes. Press START/STOP to begin cooking (The unit will steam for 10 minutes before crisping).
5. After 20 minutes, open the door and flip the lamb. Close the door to continue cooking.
6. When cooking is complete, remove the pan from the unit, slice, and serve with roasted vegetables.

Crispy Duck Breast with Orange Sauce

🕐 *Prep Time: 10 minutes, Cook Time: 20 minutes, Serves: 4*

🏆 **INGREDIENTS:**

- 4 duck breasts
- 1 tbsp. olive oil
- Salt and pepper, to taste
- 1 orange, juiced
- 1 tbsp. honey
- 1 tbsp. balsamic vinegar

🍳 **DIRECTIONS:**

1. Place the Crisper Plate in the Combi Pan and set aside.
2. Close the door and flip the SmartSwitch to AIR FRY/HOB.
3. Select AIR FRY, set temperature to 200°C and set time to 25 minutes. Press START/STOP to begin preheating (The unit will preheat for 5 minutes).
4. While the unit is preheating, score the skin of the duck breasts and season with salt and pepper.
5. Rub the duck breasts with olive oil, then place them on the Crisper Plate, skin side up.
6. When preheating is complete, open the door and slide the pan into Level 1. Close the door to continue cooking.
7. Meanwhile, combine the orange juice, honey, and balsamic vinegar in a small saucepan. Simmer over low heat until the sauce thickens.
8. When cooking is complete, remove the pan and rest the duck for 5 minutes.
9. Slice the duck breasts, drizzle with orange sauce, and serve with mashed potatoes and sautéed greens.

Grilled Rib-eye Steak with Garlic Butter

🕐 *Prep Time: 5 minutes, Cook Time: 8 minutes, Serves: 2*

🏆 **INGREDIENTS:**

- 2 rib-eye steaks
- 2 tbsps. unsalted butter, melted
- 2 cloves garlic, minced
- 1 tbsp. fresh parsley, chopped
- Salt and pepper, to taste

🍳 **DIRECTIONS:**

1. Season rib-eye steaks with salt and pepper.
2. Add steaks to the Bake Tray and slide the tray into Level 2.
3. Close the door and flip the SmartSwitch to AIR FRY/HOB. Select GRILL and set time to 8 minutes. Press START/STOP to begin cooking.
4. With 4 minutes remaining, open the door and flip the steaks. Close the door to continue cooking.
5. Meanwhile, mix the butter, garlic and parsley in a bowl.
6. When cooking is complete, remove the tray from the unit. Drizzle garlic butter over the steaks and serve with roasted potatoes or a green salad.

Bangers and Mash with Onion Gravy

🕐 *Prep Time: 10 minutes, Cook Time: 25 minutes, Serves: 4*

🏆 **INGREDIENTS:**
- 40 g butter, divided
- 8 sausages (your choice of flavour)
- 1 onion, sliced
- 500 g potatoes, peeled and chopped
- 200 ml beef stock
- 1 tbsp. plain flour
- Salt and pepper to taste

🍳 **DIRECTIONS:**
1. Side the Combi Pan into Level 1. With the door open, flip the SmartSwitch to AIRFRY/HOB. Select SEAR/SAUTÉ and set the temperature to Hi5. Press START/STOP and let the pan preheat in the unit for 2 minutes.
2. After 2 minutes, using an oven mitt, carefully remove the pan, add 15 g butter, and let it melt. Then add the sausages, return the pan to the unit and brown them for 6 minutes, turning occasionally.
3. After 6 minutes, remove the pan, set the sausages aside, and add the sliced onion to the pan. Stir fry for 3 minutes until softened.
4. After 3 minutes, sprinkle the flour over the onions, stir to combine. Return the pan to the unit and cook for 2 minutes. Add the beef stock, stirring constantly until the gravy thickens. Return the sausages to the pan, reduce the heat, and cook for 5 more minutes.
5. While the sausages and gravy cook, boil the potatoes in a separate pan for 15 minutes until tender. Mash with the remaining butter, salt, and pepper.
6. Press START/STOP to turn off the unit, serve the sausages and mash with the onion gravy.

Seared Pork Tenderloin with Apple and Sage

🕐 *Prep Time: 10 minutes, Cook Time: 18 minutes, Serves: 4*

🏆 **INGREDIENTS:**
- 25 ml olive oil
- 500 g pork tenderloin
- 1 apple, cored and sliced
- 1 tbsp. fresh sage, chopped
- 1 tbsp. Dijon mustard
- 1 tbsp. balsamic vinegar
- Salt and pepper to taste

🍳 **DIRECTIONS:**
1. Side the Combi Pan into Level 1. With the door open, flip the SmartSwitch to AIRFRY/HOB. Select SEAR/SAUTÉ and set the temperature to Hi5. Press START/STOP and let the pan preheat for 2 minutes.
2. After 2 minutes, using an oven mitt, carefully remove the pan and add the olive oil. Once hot, add the pork tenderloin. Return the pan to the unit and sear for 4-5 minutes on each side until browned.
3. After searing, remove the pan and add the apple slices and sage. Return the pan to the unit and cook for 3-4 minutes.
4. After 3-4 minutes, add the Dijon mustard, balsamic vinegar, salt and pepper. Stir to coat the pork and apples, then cook for another 5 minutes.
5. Press START/STOP to turn off the unit, remove the pan. Serve warm with mashed potatoes or steamed greens.

Sticky Chicken Thighs with Honey and Mustard

Prep Time: 5 minutes, Cook Time: 20 minutes, Serves: 4

INGREDIENTS:

- 25 g butter
- 4 chicken thighs, skin-on
- 2 tbsps. honey
- 2 tbsps. Dijon mustard
- 1 tbsp. soy sauce
- 1 tbsp. olive oil
- Salt and pepper to taste

DIRECTIONS:

1. Side the Combi Pan into Level 1. With the door open, flip the SmartSwitch to AIRFRY/HOB. Select SEAR/SAUTÉ and set the temperature to Hi5. Press START/STOP and let the pan preheat in the unit for 2 minutes.
2. After 2 minutes, using an oven mitt, carefully remove the pan, add the butter, and let it melt. Then add the chicken thighs, skin-side down, return the pan to the unit and brown for 5 minutes, turning occasionally.
3. After 5 minutes, remove the pan, add the honey, Dijon mustard, soy sauce, salt, pepper, and olive oil. Stir to combine and coat the chicken. Return the pan to the unit, reduce heat to 3, and cook for 15 minutes, turning the chicken halfway through.
4. Press START/STOP to turn off the unit, remove the pan, check the chicken is cooked through, and serve warm.

Beef and Ale Stew

Prep Time: 15 minutes, Cook Time: 5 hours on high, Serves: 4-6

INGREDIENTS:

- 500 g diced beef
- 1 onion, finely chopped
- 2 carrots, peeled and sliced
- 1 parsnip, peeled and chopped
- 300 ml ale
- 200 ml beef stock
- 1 tbsp. tomato purée
- 1 tbsp. plain flour
- 2 sprigs fresh thyme
- Salt and freshly ground black pepper to taste

DIRECTIONS:

1. Mix all the ingredients in the Combi Pan and combine well. Slide the Combi Pan into Level 1.
2. Close the door and flip the SmartSwitch to AIR FRY/HOB. Select SLOW COOK, set temperature to HIGH and set time to 5 hours. Press START/STOP to begin cooking, until the beef is tender and the vegetables are cooked through.
3. When cooking is complete, remove the pan and serve hot with crusty bread.

Grilled Halloumi and Vegetable Skewers

🕐 *Prep Time: 10 minutes, Cook Time: 10 minutes, Serves: 4*

🏆 **INGREDIENTS:**
- 200 g halloumi cheese, cut into cubes
- 1 red pepper, cut into chunks
- 1 courgette, sliced
- 1 onion, cut into wedges
- 2 tbsps. olive oil
- 1 tsp. dried oregano
- Salt and pepper, to taste

🍴 **DIRECTIONS:**
1. Thread the halloumi, red pepper, courgette, and onion alternately onto skewers. Brush with olive oil and sprinkle with oregano, salt, and pepper.
2. Place the skewers on the Bake Tray and slide the tray into Level 2.
3. Close the door and flip the SmartSwitch to AIR FRY/HOB. Select GRILL and set time to 10 minutes. Press START/STOP to begin cooking.
4. After 5 minutes, open the door and flip the skewers for even grilling.
5. When cooking is complete, remove the tray from the unit and serve with couscous or a side salad.

Traditional Lamb Hotpot

🕐 *Prep Time: 20 minutes, Cook Time: 8 hours on low, Serves: 6-8*

🏆 **INGREDIENTS:**
- 500 g lamb shoulder, diced
- 2 onions, sliced
- 2 carrots, peeled and chopped
- 600 g potatoes, thinly sliced
- 500 ml lamb stock
- 2 sprigs rosemary
- Salt and pepper to taste

🍴 **DIRECTIONS:**
1. Layer the lamb, onions, carrots, and potatoes in the Combi Pan, seasoning each layer with salt and pepper. Pour the lamb stock over the top and tuck in the rosemary sprigs.
2. Slide the Combi Pan into Level 1. Close the door and flip the SmartSwitch to AIR FRY/HOB. Select SLOW COOK, set temperature to LOW and set time to 8 hours. Press START/STOP to begin cooking, until the lamb is tender and the potatoes are fully cooked.
3. When cooking is complete, remove the pan and serve hot.

Beef Brisket with Horseradish Sauce

🕐 *Prep Time: 15 minutes, Cook Time: 70 minutes, Serves: 6*

🏆 INGREDIENTS:

- 1 kg beef brisket
- 2 tbsps. olive oil
- 2 tsps. smoked paprika
- 2 tsps. dried thyme
- 1 tsp. garlic powder
- Salt and pepper, to taste
- 1 tbsp. Dijon mustard

For the Horseradish Sauce:
- 2 tbsps. grated horseradish
- 2 tbsps. sour cream
- 1 tsp. Dijon mustard
- Salt and pepper, to taste

🍳 DIRECTIONS:

1. Place the Crisper Plate in the Combi Pan and set aside.
2. Close the door and flip the SmartSwitch to AIR FRY/HOB.
3. Select AIR FRY, set temperature to 180°C and set time to 75 minutes. Press START/STOP to begin preheating (The unit will preheat for 5 minutes).
4. While the unit is preheating, rub the beef brisket with olive oil, paprika, thyme, mustard, garlic powder, salt, and pepper.
5. When preheating is complete, open the door and place the brisket onto the Crisper Plate. Slide the pan into Level 1. Close the door to continue cooking.
6. With 30 minutes remaining, open the door and flip the brisket. Close the door to continue cooking, until the beef is tender.
7. While the beef is cooking, prepare the horseradish sauce by combining grated horseradish, sour cream, mustard, salt, and pepper in a bowl.
8. When cooking is complete, remove the pan and let the brisket rest for 10 minutes before slicing.
9. Serve the brisket with the horseradish sauce and your choice of sides, such as roast potatoes and vegetables.

Classic Roast Chicken with Root Vegetables

🕐 *Prep Time: 15 minutes, Cook Time: 60 minutes, Serves: 6*

🏆 INGREDIENTS:

- 1 whole chicken (about 1.5 kg)
- 2 medium carrots, peeled and cut into chunks
- 2 medium parsnips, peeled and cut into chunks
- 2 tbsps. olive oil
- 2 tsps. dried thyme
- 2 tsps. garlic powder
- Salt and pepper, to taste

🍳 DIRECTIONS:

1. Place the Crisper Plate in the Combi Pan and set aside.
2. Close the door and flip the SmartSwitch to AIR FRY/HOB.
3. Select AIR FRY, set temperature to 200°C and set time to 65 minutes. Press START/STOP to begin preheating (The unit will preheat for 5 minutes).
4. While the unit is preheating, rub the chicken with olive oil, thyme, garlic powder, salt, and pepper. Toss the carrots and parsnips with a drizzle of olive oil, a pinch of salt, and pepper.
5. Arrange the chicken breast-side up on the Crisper Plate, with vegetables spread around it.
6. When preheating is complete, open the door and slide the pan into Level 1. Close the door to continue cooking.
7. When 30 minutes remain, open the door and toss the vegetables. Close the door to continue cooking.
8. When cooking is complete, remove the pan. Allow the chicken to rest for 10 minutes before carving. Serve hot with the roasted vegetables.

CHAPTER 6: SEASONAL VEGETABLES & SIDES

Roasted Asparagus with Lemon and Parmesan

🕐 *Prep: 10 minutes, Total Cook Time: 24 minutes, Steam: approx. 10 minutes, Cook: 14 minutes, Serves: 4*

INGREDIENTS:
- 1 bunch of asparagus, trimmed
- 1 tbsp. olive oil
- Zest of 1 lemon
- 30 g Parmesan cheese, grated
- Salt and pepper to taste
- 120 ml water, for steaming

DIRECTIONS:
1. Pour 120 ml water in the Combi Pan for steaming, then slide the pan into Level 1.
2. Arrange the asparagus on the Bake Tray. Drizzle with olive oil, sprinkle with salt and pepper. Slide tray into Level 2.
3. Close the door and flip the SmartSwitch to COMBI COOKER. Select COMBI CRISP, set temperature to 205°C and set time to 14 minutes. Press START/STOP to (The unit will steam for 10 minutes before crisping).
4. When 5 minutes remain, open the door and sprinkle with lemon zest and Parmesan cheese. Toss to ensure an even coating. Close the door to continue cooking.
5. When cooking is complete, remove the tray from the unit and serve.

Steamed Garlic Butter Broccoli

🕐 *Prep Time: 5 minutes, Cook Time: 6 minutes, Serves: 2-3*

INGREDIENTS:
- 300 g broccoli florets
- 25 g butter, melted
- 1 clove garlic, minced
- Salt and freshly ground black pepper to taste
- 240 ml water, for steaming

DIRECTIONS:
1. Pour 240 ml water into the Combi Pan for steaming and place the Crisper Plate on top.
2. Arrange the broccoli florets evenly on the Crisper Plate and slide into level 1.
3. Close the door and flip the SmartSwitch to COMBI COOKER. Select STEAM and set the time to 6 minutes. Press START/STOP to begin cooking.
4. When cooking is complete, remove the pan from the unit. Toss the broccoli with butter, minced garlic, salt, and pepper before serving.

Crispy Parmesan Courgettes

Prep: 10 minutes, Total Cook Time: 20 minutes, Steam: approx. 6 minutes, Cook: 14 minutes, Serves: 4-6

INGREDIENTS:

- 4 medium courgettes, sliced into rounds
- 50 g breadcrumbs
- 30 g Parmesan cheese, grated
- 1 tbsp. olive oil
- Salt and pepper to taste
- 120 ml water, for steaming

DIRECTIONS:

1. Pour 120 ml water in the Combi Pan for steaming, then slide the pan into Level 1.
2. Arrange the courgette slices on the Bake Tray. Drizzle with olive oil and sprinkle with salt and pepper. Slide tray into Level 2.
3. Close the door and flip the SmartSwitch to COMBI COOKER. Select COMBI CRISP, set temperature to 205°C and set time to 14 minutes. Press START/STOP to (The unit will steam for 6 minutes before crisping).
4. When 6 minutes remain, open the door and sprinkle the courgettes with breadcrumbs and Parmesan cheese. Toss them to ensure an even coating. Close the door to continue cooking.
5. When cooking is complete, remove the tray from the unit and serve.

Roasted Pumpkin with Sage and Nutmeg

Prep: 10 minutes, Total Cook Time: 26 minutes, Steam: approx. 8 minutes, Cook: 18 minutes, Serves: 4

INGREDIENTS:

- 500 g pumpkin, peeled and cut into chunks
- 1 tbsp. olive oil
- 1 tsp. dried sage
- ½ tsp. ground nutmeg
- Salt and pepper to taste
- 120 ml water, for steaming

DIRECTIONS:

1. Pour 120 ml water in the Combi Pan for steaming, then slide the pan into Level 1.
2. Arrange the pumpkin chunks on the Bake Tray. Drizzle with olive oil, sprinkle with sage, nutmeg, salt, and pepper. Slide tray into Level 2.
3. Close the door and flip the SmartSwitch to COMBI COOKER. Select COMBI CRISP, set temperature to 200°C and set time to 18 minutes. Press START/STOP to (The unit will steam for 8 minutes before crisping).
4. When 9 minutes remain, open the door and toss the pumpkin to ensure even cooking. Close the door to continue cooking.
5. When cooking is complete, remove the tray from the unit and serve.

Chickpea and Spinach Stir-Fry

Prep Time: 10 minutes, Cook Time: 8 minutes, Serves: 4

INGREDIENTS:

- 25 ml olive oil
- 1 can (400 g) chickpeas, drained and rinsed
- 1 onion, sliced
- 2 cloves garlic, minced
- 100 g spinach
- 1 tsp. cumin
- 1 tsp. paprika
- Salt and pepper to taste

DIRECTIONS:

1. Side the Combi Pan into Level 1. With the door open, flip the SmartSwitch to AIRFRY/HOB. Select SEAR/SAUTÉ and set the temperature to Hi5. Press START/STOP and let the pan preheat for 2 minutes.
2. After 2 minutes, using an oven mitt, carefully remove the pan and add the olive oil. Once hot, add the onion and garlic, return the pan to the unit and sauté for 3 minutes until softened.
3. After 3 minutes, add the chickpeas, cumin, paprika, salt and pepper, then return the pan to the unit. Stir to combine and cook for 3 minutes.
4. After 3 minutes, remove the pan and add the spinach, stirring for 2 minutes until it wilts.
5. Press START/STOP to turn off the unit, remove the pan. Serve warm with a side of rice or flatbreads.

Mustard Cauliflower with Cheddar

Prep Time: 10 minutes, Cook Time: 15 minutes, Serves: 4

INGREDIENTS:

- 1 small cauliflower, cut into florets
- 1 tbsp. olive oil
- 50 g mature cheddar cheese, grated
- 1 tsp. Dijon mustard
- Salt and pepper to taste

DIRECTIONS:

1. Place the Crisper Plate in the Combi Pan and set aside.
2. Close the door and flip the SmartSwitch to AIR FRY/HOB.
3. Select AIR FRY, set temperature to 200°C and set time to 20 minutes. Press START/STOP to begin preheating (The unit will preheat for 5 minutes).
4. While the unit is preheating, toss the cauliflower florets with olive oil, mustard, salt, and pepper in a bowl. Place the cauliflower onto the Crisper Plate.
5. When 15 minutes remain, open the door and slide the pan into Level 1. Close the door to continue cooking.
6. When 5 minutes remain, sprinkle the grated cheddar over the cauliflower. Close the door to continue cooking.
7. When cooking is complete, remove the pan and serve the cauliflower hot.

Beetroot with Feta and Walnuts

🕐 *Prep Time: 10 minutes, Cook Time: 20 minutes, Serves: 4*

🍽 INGREDIENTS:
- 4 medium beetroots, peeled and cut into wedges
- 1 tbsp. olive oil
- 50 g feta cheese, crumbled
- 30 g walnuts, chopped
- Salt and pepper to taste

🍳 DIRECTIONS:
1. Place the Crisper Plate in the Combi Pan and set aside.
2. Close the door and flip the SmartSwitch to AIR FRY/HOB.
3. Select AIR FRY, set temperature to 180°C and set time to 25 minutes. Press START/STOP to begin preheating (The unit will preheat for 5 minutes).
4. While the unit is preheating, toss the beetroot wedges with olive oil, salt, and pepper in a bowl. Place the beetroot wedges onto the Crisper Plate.
5. When 20 minutes remain, open the door and slide the pan into Level 1. Close the door to continue cooking.
6. When 10 minutes remain, open the door and toss the beetroot wedges. Close the door to continue cooking.
7. When cooking is complete, remove the pan, top with crumbled feta and chopped walnuts, and serve.

Creamy Potato and Leek Soup

🕐 *Prep Time: 10 minutes, Cook Time: 6 hours on low, Serves: 4-6*

🍽 INGREDIENTS:
- 3 large leeks, washed and sliced
- 400 g potatoes, peeled and diced
- 1 onion, chopped
- 800 ml vegetable stock
- 150 ml single cream
- 25 g butter
- Salt and pepper to taste

🍳 DIRECTIONS:
1. Mix the leeks, potatoes, onion, butter, and stock in the Combi Pan and combine well. Slide the Combi Pan into Level 1.
2. Close the door and flip the SmartSwitch to AIR FRY/HOB. Select SLOW COOK, set temperature to LOW and set time to 6 hours. Press START/STOP to begin cooking.
3. When cooking is complete, blend the soup until smooth. Stir in the cream, season with salt and pepper, and serve hot.

Honey Glazed Roast Carrots with Mustard Seeds

🕐 *Prep: 10 minutes, Total Cook Time: 30 minutes, Steam: approx. 8 minutes, Cook: 22 minutes, Serves: 4-6*

🏆 **INGREDIENTS:**
- 6 medium carrots, peeled and cut into sticks
- 1 tbsp. honey
- 1 tsp. mustard seeds
- 1 tbsp. olive oil
- Salt and pepper to taste
- 120 ml water, for steaming

🍳 **DIRECTIONS:**
1. Pour 120 ml water in the Combi Pan for steaming, then slide the pan into Level 1.
2. Arrange the carrot sticks on the Bake Tray. Drizzle with olive oil, and sprinkle with salt and pepper. Slide tray into Level 2.
3. Close the door and flip the SmartSwitch to COMBI COOKER. Select COMBI CRISP, set temperature to 200°C and set time to 22 minutes. Press START/STOP to (The unit will steam for 8 minutes before crisping).
4. When 10 minutes remain, open the door and drizzle honey over the carrots and sprinkle with mustard seeds. Toss the carrots to coat. Close the door to continue cooking.
5. When cooking is complete, remove the tray from the unit and serve.

Thyme Sweet Potato Wedges

🕐 *Prep Time: 10 minutes, Cook Time: 20 minutes, Serves: 4*

🏆 **INGREDIENTS:**
- 2 large sweet potatoes, peeled and cut into wedges
- 1 tbsp. olive oil
- 1 tsp. fresh thyme, chopped
- 1 tbsp. honey
- Salt and pepper to taste

🍳 **DIRECTIONS:**
1. Place the Crisper Plate in the Combi Pan and set aside.
2. Close the door and flip the SmartSwitch to AIR FRY/HOB.
3. Select AIR FRY, set temperature to 200°C and set time to 25 minutes. Press START/STOP to begin preheating (The unit will preheat for 5 minutes).
4. While the unit is preheating, toss the sweet potato wedges with olive oil, thyme, honey, salt, and pepper in a bowl. Place the sweet potato wedges onto the Crisper Plate.
5. When 20 minutes remain, open the door and slide the pan into Level 1. Close the door to continue cooking.
6. When 10 minutes remain, open the door and toss the wedges. Close the door to continue cooking.
7. When cooking is complete, remove the pan and serve the sweet potato wedges.

Steamed Minted New Potatoes

🕐 *Prep Time: 5 minutes, Cook Time: 15 minutes, Serves: 4*

🍷 **INGREDIENTS:**
- 500 g baby new potatoes
- 2 sprigs fresh mint
- 25 g butter, melted
- Salt to taste
- 300 ml water, for steaming

🍳 **DIRECTIONS:**
1. Pour 300 ml water into the Combi Pan for steaming and place the Crisper Plate on top.
2. Arrange the new potatoes evenly on the Crisper Plate and tuck the mint sprigs among them. And slide into level 1.
3. Close the door and flip the SmartSwitch to COMBI COOKER. Select STEAM and set the time to 15 minutes. Press START/STOP to begin cooking.
4. When cooking is complete, remove the pan from the unit. Discard the mint sprigs, toss the potatoes with butter and salt, and serve.

Buttery Mushrooms with Garlic and Thyme

🕐 *Prep: 10 minutes, Total Cook Time: 20 minutes, Steam: approx. 8 minutes, Cook: 12 minutes, Serves: 2-3*

🍷 **INGREDIENTS:**
- 250 g button mushrooms, cleaned and halved
- 1 tbsp. butter, melted
- 2 garlic cloves, minced
- 1 tsp. fresh thyme, chopped
- Salt and pepper to taste
- 120 ml water, for steaming

🍳 **DIRECTIONS:**
1. Pour 120 ml water in the Combi Pan for steaming, then slide the pan into Level 1.
2. Arrange the mushrooms on the Bake Tray. Drizzle with melted butter, sprinkle with minced garlic, thyme, salt, and pepper. Slide tray into Level 2.
3. Close the door and flip the SmartSwitch to COMBI COOKER. Select COMBI CRISP, set temperature to 200°C and set time to 12 minutes. Press START/STOP to (The unit will steam for 8 minutes before crisping).
4. When 6 minutes remain, open the door and toss the mushrooms. Close the door to continue cooking.
5. When cooking is complete, remove the tray from the unit and serve.

CHAPTER 7: SEAFOOD SPECIALTIES

Steamed Lemon Herb Salmon

Prep Time: 5 minutes, Cook Time: 10 minutes, Serves: 2

INGREDIENTS:
- 2 salmon fillets (approx. 150 g each)
- 1 lemon, sliced
- 1 tbsp. fresh dill, chopped
- 1 tbsp. olive oil
- Salt and freshly ground black pepper to taste
- 240 ml water, for steaming

DIRECTIONS:
1. Pour 240 ml water into the Combi Pan for steaming and place the Crisper Plate on top.
2. Season the salmon fillets with salt, pepper, and olive oil. Sprinkle dill on top and arrange lemon slices over the salmon.
3. Place the fillets on the Crisper Plate and slide into level 1.
4. Close the door and flip the SmartSwitch to COMBI COOKER. Select STEAM and set the time to 10 minutes. Press START/STOP to begin cooking, until the fish flakes easily with a fork.
5. When cooking is complete, remove the pan from the unit. Plate the salmon with lemon slices and serve immediately.

Grilled Prawn Skewers with Lime and Coriander

Prep Time: 10 minutes, Cook Time: 8 minutes, Serves: 4

INGREDIENTS:
- 20 large prawns, peeled and deveined
- 2 tbsps. olive oil
- Juice and zest of 1 lime
- 1 tsp. fresh ginger, grated
- 1 red chilli, finely chopped
- Salt and pepper to taste
- 4 wooden skewers, soaked in water for 30 minutes
- Fresh coriander, chopped, for garnish

DIRECTIONS:
1. Mix olive oil, lime juice, lime zest, ginger, chilli, salt, and pepper in a small bowl to make the marinade. Brush the prawns generously with the marinade.
2. Thread five prawns onto each skewer. Add the skewers to the Bake Tray and slide the tray into Level 2.
3. Close the door and flip the SmartSwitch to AIR FRY/HOB. Select GRILL and set the time to 8 minutes. Press START/STOP to begin cooking.
4. After 4 minutes, open the door and flip the skewers. Close the door and continue grilling.
5. When cooking is complete, remove the skewers and garnish with fresh coriander. Serve immediately.

Battered Prawns with Garlic Mayonnaise

🕐 *Prep Time: 15 minutes, Cook Time: 9 minutes, Serves: 4*

🦐 **INGREDIENTS:**
- Cooking spray
- 16 large prawns, peeled and deveined
- 80 g plain flour
- 1 egg, beaten
- 60 g breadcrumbs
- 60 g butter, melted
- 1 garlic clove, minced
- 2 tbsps. mayonnaise
- Lemon wedge for serving

🍳 **DIRECTIONS:**
1. Add the melted butter, minced garlic and stir in the mayonnaise to create the garlic mayonnaise sauce.
2. Coat the prawns in flour, dip them in the beaten egg, and then coat with breadcrumbs. Lightly spray with cooking spray.
3. Place the Crisper Plate in the Combi Pan and set aside.
4. Close door and flip the SmartSwitch to AIR FRY/HOB.
5. Select AIR FRY, set temperature to 205°C and set time to 14 minutes. Press START/STOP to begin preheating (The unit will preheat for 5 minutes).
6. While the unit is preheating, place the prawns onto the Crisper Plate.
7. When 9 minutes remain on the timer, open the door and slide the pan into Level 1. Close the door to continue cooking.
8. When 4 minutes remain, open the door and toss the prawns. Close the door to continue cooking.
9. When cooking is complete, remove the pan and serve the prawns with garlic mayonnaise and a wedge of lemon.

Lobster Tails with Herbed Butter

🕐 *Prep Time: 10 minutes, Cook Time: 10 minutes, Serves: 2*

🦐 **INGREDIENTS:**
- 2 lobster tails, halved
- 50 g unsalted butter, melted
- 2 garlic cloves, minced
- 1 tsp. fresh thyme leaves
- 1 tsp. smoked paprika
- Juice of ½ lemon
- Salt and pepper to taste
- Fresh chives, chopped, for garnish

🍳 **DIRECTIONS:**
1. Add the lobster tails to the Bake Tray and slide the tray into Level 2.
2. Close the door and flip the SmartSwitch to AIR FRY/HOB. Select GRILL and set time to 10 minutes. Press START/STOP to begin cooking.
3. While the lobster is grilling, mix melted butter, garlic, thyme, smoked paprika, lemon juice, salt, and pepper in a bowl.
4. After 5 minutes, open the door and brush the butter mixture generously over the lobster tails. Close the door and continue grilling.
5. When cooking is complete, garnish with chives and serve immediately.

Mussels in Garlic Butter

Prep: 10 minutes, Total Cook Time: 20 minutes, Steam: approx. 10 minutes, Cook: 10 minutes, Serves: 4

INGREDIENTS:
- 500 g mussels, cleaned
- 1 tbsp. butter, melted
- 2 garlic cloves, minced
- 1 tbsp. fresh parsley, chopped
- 1 tbsp. lemon juice
- Salt and pepper to taste
- 240 ml water, for steaming

DIRECTIONS:
1. In a small bowl, mix the melted butter with garlic, parsley, lemon juice, salt, and pepper. Drizzle the garlic butter over the mussels.
2. Pour 240 ml water in the Combi Pan for steaming, then slide the pan into Level 1.
3. Arrange the mussels on the Bake Tray. Slide tray into Level 2.
4. Close the door and flip the SmartSwitch to COMBI COOKER. Select COMBI CRISP, set temperature to 205°C and set time to 10 minutes. Press START/STOP to (The unit will steam for 10 minutes before crisping).
5. When cooking is complete, remove the pan from the unit and serve the mussels with crusty bread.

Grilled Garlic Oysters with Parsley

Prep Time: 10 minutes, Cook Time: 6 minutes, Serves: 4

INGREDIENTS:
- 8 large oysters, shucked
- 50 g Parmesan cheese, grated
- 2 garlic cloves, minced
- 2 tbsps. unsalted butter, melted
- Salt and pepper to taste
- Fresh parsley, chopped, for garnish

DIRECTIONS:
1. Add the shucked oysters to the Bake Tray and slide the tray into Level 2.
2. Close the door and flip the SmartSwitch to AIR FRY/HOB. Select GRILL and set time to 6 minutes. Press START/STOP to begin cooking.
3. While the oysters are grilling, mix Parmesan cheese, garlic, melted butter, salt, and pepper in a bowl.
4. After 3 minutes, open the door and spoon the mixture over each oyster. Close the door and continue grilling.
5. When cooking is complete, garnish with parsley and serve hot.

Salmon Stir-Fry with Asparagus and Spinach

🕐 *Prep Time: 10 minutes, Cook Time: 11 minutes, Serves: 4-6*

🏆 **INGREDIENTS:**

- 25 ml olive oil
- 500 g salmon fillets, skin removed, cut into chunks
- 150 g asparagus, chopped
- 100 g spinach
- 2 tbsps. soy sauce
- 1 tbsp. lemon juice
- 1 tsp. dill, plus more for garnish
- Salt and pepper to taste

🍲 **DIRECTIONS:**

❶ Side the Combi Pan into Level 1. With the door open, flip the SmartSwitch to AIRFRY/HOB. Select SEAR/SAUTÉ and set the temperature to Hi5. Press START/STOP and let the pan preheat for 2 minutes.

❷ After 2 minutes, using an oven mitt, carefully remove the pan and add the olive oil. Once hot, add the salmon chunks, return the pan to the unit and cook for 6 minutes until browned.

❸ After browning, remove the pan and add the asparagus and spinach. Return the pan to the unit and stir-fry for another 3 minutes, ensuring the spinach wilts and the asparagus is tender.

❹ After 3 minutes, add the soy sauce, lemon juice, dill, salt and pepper. Stir to combine and cook for another 2 minutes.

❺ Press START/STOP to turn off the unit, remove the pan. Serve warm, garnished with extra dill if desired.

Crab Cakes with Lemon and Dill

🕐 *Prep: 20 minutes, Total Cook Time: 16 minutes, Steam: approx. 6 minutes, Cook: 10 minutes, Serves: 4*

🏆 **INGREDIENTS:**

- Cooking spray
- 200 g white crab meat
- 1 egg
- 2 tbsps. breadcrumbs
- 1 tbsp. mayonnaise
- 1 tsp. Dijon mustard
- 1 tbsp. fresh dill, chopped, plus more for serving
- 1 tsp. lemon juice
- Salt and pepper to taste
- A dollop of sour cream, for serving
- 240 ml water, for steaming

🍲 **DIRECTIONS:**

❶ In a bowl, mix together crab meat, egg, breadcrumbs, mayonnaise, mustard, dill, lemon juice, salt, and pepper. Form into small cakes. Lightly spray with cooking spray.

❷ Pour 240 ml water in the Combi Pan for steaming, then slide the pan into Level 1.

❸ Arrange the crab cakes on the Bake Tray. Slide tray into Level 2.

❹ Close the door and flip the SmartSwitch to COMBI COOKER. Select COMBI CRISP, set temperature to 205°C and set time to 10 minutes. Press START/STOP to (The unit will steam for 6 minutes before crisping).

❺ When 5 minutes remain, open the door and flip the crab cakes. Close the door to continue cooking.

❻ When cooking is complete, remove the tray from the unit and serve with a dollop of sour cream and a sprinkle of fresh dill.

Grilled Whole Trout with Lemon

🕐 *Prep Time: 15 minutes, Cook Time: 14 minutes, Serves: 2-4*

🍸 **INGREDIENTS:**
- 2 whole trout (about 400 g each), gutted and cleaned
- 2 garlic cloves, minced
- 1 tsp. smoked paprika
- 1 tsp. dried oregano
- 1 tbsp. olive oil
- 1 lemon, sliced
- Salt and pepper to taste
- Fresh parsley, chopped, for garnish

🍽 **DIRECTIONS:**
1. Add the trout to the Bake Tray and slide the tray into Level 2.
2. Close the door and flip the SmartSwitch to AIR FRY/HOB. Select GRILL and set time to 14 minutes. Press START/STOP to begin cooking.
3. While the fish is grilling, mix garlic, smoked paprika, oregano, olive oil, salt, and pepper in a bowl into a paste.
4. After 7 minutes, open the door and spread the paste evenly over the trout. Add lemon slices on top. Close the door and continue grilling.
5. When cooking is complete, garnish with parsley and serve immediately.

Traditional Steamed Haddock with Peas

🕐 *Prep Time: 5 minutes, Cook Time: 8 minutes, Serves: 2*

🍸 **INGREDIENTS:**
- 2 haddock fillets (approx. 150 g each)
- 150 g frozen peas
- 1 tbsp. butter, melted
- 1 tsp. fresh mint, chopped
- Salt and freshly ground black pepper to taste
- 240 ml water, for steaming

🍽 **DIRECTIONS:**
1. Pour 240 ml water into the Combi Pan for steaming and place the Crisper Plate on top.
2. Place the haddock fillets on one side of the Crisper Plate and frozen peas on the other. Slide into level 1.
3. Close the door and flip the SmartSwitch to COMBI COOKER. Select STEAM and set the time to 8 minutes. Press START/STOP to begin cooking.
4. When cooking is complete, remove the pan from the unit. Mix butter and mint with the peas, season the haddock with salt and pepper, and serve.

Baked Cod with Parsley Crust

🕐 *Prep: 15 minutes, Total Cook Time: 18 minutes, Steam: approx. 8 minutes, Cook: 10 minutes, Serves: 4*

🍴 **INGREDIENTS:**
- Cooking spray
- 4 cod fillets
- 100 g fresh breadcrumbs
- 2 tbsps. fresh parsley, chopped
- 2 tbsps. olive oil
- 2 tsps. lemon zest
- Salt and pepper to taste
- 240 ml water, for steaming

🍳 **DIRECTIONS:**
1. In a bowl, combine breadcrumbs, parsley, olive oil, lemon zest, salt, and pepper. Press the mixture onto the top of the cod fillets. Lightly spray with cooking spray.
2. Pour 240 ml water in the Combi Pan for steaming, then slide the pan into Level 1.
3. Arrange the cod fillets on the Bake Tray. Slide tray into Level 2.
4. Close the door and flip the SmartSwitch to COMBI COOKER. Select COMBI CRISP, set temperature to 205°C and set time to 10 minutes. Press START/STOP to (The unit will steam for 8 minutes before crisping).
5. When cooking is complete, remove the pan from the unit and serve with steamed vegetables.

Chilli Scallops with Coriander

🕐 *Prep Time: 10 minutes, Cook Time: 6 minutes, Serves: 4*

🍴 **INGREDIENTS:**
- 400 g fresh scallops, cleaned
- 1 tbsp. olive oil
- 1 red chilli, finely chopped
- 2 garlic cloves, minced
- Juice of 1 lemon
- Salt and pepper to taste
- Fresh coriander, chopped, for garnish

🍳 **DIRECTIONS:**
1. Mix olive oil, chilli, garlic, lemon juice, salt, and pepper in a small bowl. Brush the scallops with the seasoning mixture.
2. Add the scallops to the Bake Tray and slide the tray into Level 2.
3. Close the door and flip the SmartSwitch to AIR FRY/HOB. Select GRILL and set time to 6 minutes. Press START/STOP to begin cooking.
4. After 3 minutes, open the door and flip the scallops. Close the door and continue grilling.
5. When cooking is complete, garnish with coriander and serve immediately.

CHAPTER 8: CELEBRATION FEASTS

Classic Scotch Eggs

Prep: 20 minutes, Total Cook Time: 22 minutes, Steam: approx. 6 minutes, Cook: 16 minutes, Serves: 4

INGREDIENTS:
- 4 sausages, skins removed
- 4 boiled eggs, peeled
- 100 g breadcrumbs
- 1 tsp. dried thyme
- 1 egg, beaten
- Salt and pepper to taste
- 120 ml water, for steaming

DIRECTIONS:
1. Pour 120 ml water into the Combi Pan for steaming and place the Crisper Plate on top.
2. Roll each boiled egg in the sausage meat, then dip in beaten egg and coat with breadcrumbs mixed with thyme, salt, and pepper.
3. Arrange the scotch eggs on the Crisper Plate. Slide the pan into Level 1.
4. Close the door and flip the SmartSwitch to COMBI COOKER. Select COMBI CRISP, set the temperature to 200°C, and set the time to 16 minutes. Press START/STOP to begin cooking (The unit will steam for 6 minutes before crisping).
5. When 10 minutes remain, open the door and flip the scotch eggs. Close the door to continue cooking.
6. When cooking is complete, remove the pan and serve the scotch eggs.

Festive Mince Pies

Prep Time: 20 minutes, Cook Time: 15 minutes, Serves: 8

INGREDIENTS:
- 8 ready-made shortcrust pastry cases
- 150 g mince meat filling (store-bought or homemade)

DIRECTIONS:
1. Place the Crisper Plate in the Combi Pan and arrange the ready-made pastry cases on the plate.
2. Fill each pastry case with mincemeat, ensuring not to overfill.
3. Flip the SmartSwitch to AIR FRY/HOB. Select BAKE, set temperature to 200°C, and set time to 18 minutes. Press START/STOP to begin preheat (The unit will preheat for 3 minutes).
4. When preheat is complete, open the door and slide the pan into Level 1. Close the door to start cooking.
5. When cooking is complete, pull the Combi Pan out, and allow to cool before serving.

Grilled Beef Burgers with Cheddar Cheese

🕐 *Prep Time: 10 minutes, Cook Time: 10 minutes, Serves: 4*

🏆 **INGREDIENTS:**
- 500 g beef mince
- 1 tbsp. olive oil
- Salt and pepper, to taste
- 1 tsp. garlic powder
- 1 tsp. onion powder
- 4 slices cheddar cheese
- 4 burger buns
- Optional: Lettuce, tomato, and ketchup for garnish

🍳 **DIRECTIONS:**
1. In a bowl, combine the beef mince, olive oil, salt, pepper, garlic powder, and onion powder. Mix until just combined. Shape the mixture into 4 even patties.
2. Add the burger patties to the Bake Tray and slide the tray into Level 2.
3. Close the door and flip the SmartSwitch to AIR FRY/HOB. Select GRILL and set the time to 10 minutes. Press START/STOP to begin cooking.
4. After 5 minutes, open the door, flip the patties and place a slice of cheddar cheese on each patty. Continue grilling until the cheese is melted and the patties are cooked through.
5. When cooking is complete, remove the tray from the unit. Serve the burgers on buns with optional toppings such as lettuce, tomato, and ketchup.

Pigs in Blankets

🕐 *Prep Time: 10 minutes, Cook Time: 12 minutes, Serves: 4*

🏆 **INGREDIENTS:**
- 12 cocktail sausages
- 12 rashers streaky bacon

🍳 **DIRECTIONS:**
1. Place the Crisper Plate in the Combi Pan and set aside.
2. Close the door and flip the SmartSwitch to AIR FRY/HOB.
3. Select AIR FRY, set temperature to 200°C, and set time to 17 minutes. Press START/STOP to begin preheating (The unit will preheat for 5 minutes).
4. While the unit is preheating, wrap each cocktail sausage with a rasher of bacon and secure with a toothpick if needed.
5. When preheating is complete, arrange the pigs in blankets on the Crisper Plate. Slide the pan into Level 1. Close the door to continue cooking.
6. When 6 minutes remain, open the door and flip the pigs in blankets. Close the door to continue cooking.
7. When cooking is complete, remove the pan and serve hot.

Steak and Kidney Pie

Prep Time: 30 minutes, Cook Time: 55 minutes, Serves: 6-8

INGREDIENTS:

- 500 g beef steak, diced
- 250 g kidney, diced
- 1 onion, chopped
- 100 g mushrooms, sliced
- 1 tbsp. flour
- 250 ml beef stock
- 1 tsp. Worcestershire sauce
- 1 pack of puff pastry
- 1 egg, beaten
- Salt and pepper

DIRECTIONS:

1. In a saucepan, heat a little oil and brown the diced beef and kidney, about 8 minutes. Add the onion and cook until soft.
2. Stir in the flour and cook for 2 minutes, then add the beef stock and Worcestershire sauce. Simmer for 15 minutes until thickened.
3. Add the sliced mushrooms, and season with salt and pepper. Continue to cook for another 5 minutes, then remove from heat.
4. Roll out the puff pastry on a floured surface to fit the size of your pie dish.
5. Line the pie dish with the rolled-out pastry, making sure it covers the bottom and sides.
6. Pour the cooked beef and kidney mixture into the pastry-lined pie dish.
7. Roll out the remaining puff pastry and use it to cover the top of the pie.
8. Seal the edges of the pastry by pressing down with your fingers or a fork.
9. Cut a few slits in the top of the pastry to allow steam to escape. Brush with the beaten egg.
10. Flip the SmartSwitch to AIR FRY/HOB. Select BAKE, set temperature to 200°C, and set time to 28 minutes. Press START/STOP to begin preheat. (The unit will preheat for 3 minutes).
11. When preheat is complete, open the door and slide the pan into Level 1. Close the door to start cooking.
12. When cooking is complete, pull the Combi Pan out, allow to rest for a few minutes before serving.

Fish and Chips

Prep Time: 15 minutes, Cook Time: 25 minutes, Serves: 2

INGREDIENTS:

- Cooking spray
- 2 white fish fillets (such as cod or haddock)
- 2 medium potatoes, peeled and cut into chips
- 2 tbsps. olive oil
- 1 tsp. paprika
- Salt and pepper
- 1 egg, beaten
- 50 g breadcrumbs
- 1 tbsp. plain flour

DIRECTIONS:

1. Place the Crisper Plate in the Combi Pan and set aside.
2. Close the door and flip the SmartSwitch to AIR FRY/HOB.
3. Select AIR FRY, set temperature to 200°C, and set time to 30 minutes. Press START/STOP to begin preheating (The unit will preheat for 5 minutes).
4. While the unit is preheating, toss the potato chips in olive oil, paprika, salt, and pepper.
5. Pat the fish fillets dry with a paper towel. Season with salt and pepper. Lightly dust each fillet with plain flour, then dip into the beaten egg, ensuring it is evenly coated. Roll the fish in breadcrumbs until fully covered. Set aside.
6. When the preheat time is complete, arrange the chips on the Crisper Plate and lightly spray with cooking spray. Slide the pan into Level 1. Close the door to continue cooking.
7. When 10 minutes remain, open the door and flip the chips. Place the fish fillets on the Crisper Plate and close the door to continue cooking.
8. When cooking is complete, remove the pan and serve hot.

Lamb Chops with Garlic and Thyme

🕐 *Prep Time: 10 minutes, Cook Time: 13 minutes, Serves: 4*

🏆 **INGREDIENTS:**
- 30 g butter
- 4 lamb chops
- 3 cloves garlic, minced
- 2 sprigs thyme, chopped
- 1 tbsp. olive oil
- Salt and pepper to taste

🍳 **DIRECTIONS:**
1. Side the Combi Pan into Level 1. With the door open, flip the SmartSwitch to AIRFRY/HOB. Select SEAR/SAUTÉ and set the temperature to 4. Press START/STOP and let the pan preheat in the unit for 2 minutes.
2. After 2 minutes, using an oven mitt, carefully remove the pan, add the butter, and let it melt. Then add the lamb chops, return the pan to the unit and brown on both sides for 4 minutes, turning the chops occasionally.
3. After browning, remove the pan, add the minced garlic, thyme, olive oil, salt and pepper, then stir. Return the pan to the unit and sauté for another 5 minutes, until the lamb is cooked through and fragrant.
4. Press START/STOP to turn off the unit, remove the pan and serve warm.

Stuffing Balls

🕐 *Prep Time: 10 minutes, Cook Time: 14 minutes, Serves: 4*

🏆 **INGREDIENTS:**
- Cooking spray
- 200 g sausage meat
- 100 g breadcrumbs
- 1 small onion, finely chopped
- 1 tbsp. fresh parsley, chopped
- Salt and pepper

🍳 **DIRECTIONS:**
1. Place the Crisper Plate in the Combi Pan and set aside.
2. Close the door and flip the SmartSwitch to AIR FRY/HOB.
3. Select AIR FRY, set temperature to 200°C, and set time to 19 minutes. Press START/STOP to begin preheating (The unit will preheat for 5 minutes).
4. While the unit is preheating, mix the sausage meat, breadcrumbs, onion, parsley, salt, and pepper in a bowl. Roll the mixture into small balls. Spray with cooking spray.
5. When the preheat time is complete, arrange the stuffing balls on the Crisper Plate. Slide the pan into Level 1. Close the door to continue cooking.
6. When 7 minutes remain, open the door and toss the balls. Close the door to continue cooking.
7. When cooking is complete, remove the pan and serve.

Crispy Pork Belly with Apple Sauce

Prep: 10 minutes, Total Cook Time: 50 minutes, Steam: approx. 10 minutes, Cook: 40 minutes, Serves: 6

INGREDIENTS:
- 1 kg pork belly
- 2 tbsps. olive oil
- 1 tsp. sea salt
- 1 tsp. black pepper
- 2 apples, peeled, cored, and chopped
- 1 tbsp. sugar
- 1 tbsp. vinegar
- 240 ml water, for steaming

DIRECTIONS:
1. Pour 240 ml of water in the Combi Pan for steaming and place the Crisper Plate on top.
2. Rub the pork belly with olive oil, sea salt, and black pepper. Place the pork belly on the Crisper Plate, skin-side up. Slide the pan into Level 1.
3. Close the door and flip the SmartSwitch to COMBI COOKER. Select COMBI CRISP, set temperature to 220°C and set time to 40 minutes. Press START/STOP to begin cooking (The unit will steam for 10 minutes before crisping).
4. After 20 minutes, open the door and check the crackling. Flip the pork belly if needed. Close the door to continue cooking.
5. While the pork is cooking, make the apple sauce: in a saucepan, cook the apples with sugar and vinegar until soft. Mash the apples into a sauce.
6. When cooking is complete, remove the pan from the unit, carve, and serve with apple sauce.

Lemon Drizzle Cake

Prep Time: 10 minutes, Cook Time: 25 minutes, Serves: 8

INGREDIENTS:
- 200 g self-raising flour
- 200 g caster sugar
- 200 g unsalted butter, softened
- 4 large eggs
- 1 lemon, zest and juice

For the Lemon Icing:
- 15 ml lemon juice
- 50 g icing sugar

DIRECTIONS:
1. Add the flour, butter, caster sugar, eggs, lemon zest, and juice to the Combi Pan. Stir well to combine and set aside.
2. Flip the SmartSwitch to AIR FRY/HOB. Select BAKE, set temperature to 180°C, and set time to 28 minutes. Press START/STOP to begin preheat. (The unit will preheat for 3 minutes).
3. When preheat is complete, open the door and slide the pan into Level 1. Close the door to start cooking.
4. When cooking is complete, pull the Combi Pan out, allow the cake to cool, then drizzle with lemon icing made from the icing sugar and lemon juice.

Mini Yorkshire Puddings

Prep Time: 10 minutes, Cook Time: 10 minutes, Serves: 6

INGREDIENTS:
- 120 g plain flour
- 2 large eggs
- 150 ml milk
- 1 tbsp. vegetable oil
- Salt and pepper

DIRECTIONS:
1. Place the Crisper Plate in the Combi Pan and set aside.
2. Close the door and flip the SmartSwitch to AIR FRY/HOB.
3. Select AIR FRY, set temperature to 210°C, and set time to 15 minutes. Press START/STOP to begin preheating (The unit will preheat for 5 minutes).
4. While the unit is preheating, whisk together the flour, eggs, milk, vegetable oil and a pinch of salt and pepper in a bowl.
5. When the preheat is complete, pour the batter into a greased muffin tin or silicone mould, filling each section halfway. Place the muffin tin into the plate.
6. Open the door and slide the pan into Level 1. Close the door to continue cooking.
7. When cooking is complete, remove the pan and allow to cool slightly before serving.

Classic Shepherd's Pie

Prep Time: 20 minutes, Cook Time: 45 minutes, Serves: 4-6

INGREDIENTS:
- 500 g minced lamb
- 1 onion, finely chopped
- 2 carrots, peeled and diced
- 2 tbsps. tomato purée
- 200 ml lamb stock
- 1 tsp. dried rosemary
- 1 tbsp. Worcestershire sauce
- Salt and pepper to taste
- 900 g potatoes, peeled and boiled
- 50 g butter
- 50 ml milk

DIRECTIONS:
1. In a saucepan, brown the minced lamb, then add the onion and carrots. Cook until softened, about 5 minutes.
2. Stir in the tomato purée, lamb stock, rosemary, and Worcestershire sauce. Simmer for 10 minutes until thickened. Season with salt and pepper.
3. Mash the boiled potatoes with butter, milk, and a pinch of salt.
4. Transfer the lamb mixture into the Combi Pan and top with the mashed potatoes.
5. Flip the SmartSwitch to AIR FRY/HOB. Select BAKE, set temperature to 200°C, and set time to 33 minutes. Press START/STOP to begin preheat. (The unit will preheat for 3 minutes).
6. When preheat is complete, open the door and slide the pan into Level 1. Close the door to start cooking.
7. When cooking is complete, pull the Combi Pan out and serve hot.

Beef Wellington Bites

🕐 *Prep Time: 15 minutes, Cook Time: 15 minutes, Serves: 4*

🏆 **INGREDIENTS:**
- Cooking spray
- 250 g beef fillet, cut into bite-sized pieces
- 100 g mushroom duxelles
- 2 tbsps. Dijon mustard
- 4 sheets puff pastry
- 1 egg, beaten
- Salt and pepper

🍳 **DIRECTIONS:**

1. Sear the beef fillet pieces in a hot pan for 2-3 minutes until browned, then remove from heat and brush with Dijon mustard. Season with salt and pepper.
2. Roll the puff pastry out and cut into squares. Place a tsp. of mushroom duxelles and a piece of beef on each pastry square, fold the edges to enclose, and seal with a beaten egg.
3. Place the Crisper Plate in the Combi Pan and set aside.
4. Close the door and flip the SmartSwitch to AIR FRY/HOB.
5. Select AIR FRY, set temperature to 200°C, and set time to 17 minutes. Press START/STOP to begin preheating (The unit will preheat for 5 minutes).
6. When preheating is complete, arrange the Wellington bites on the Crisper Plate and spray with cooking spray. Slide the pan into Level 1. Close the door to continue cooking.
7. When cooking is complete, remove the pan and serve hot.

Classic British Vegetable Stew

🕐 *Prep Time: 15 minutes, Cook Time: 4 hours on high, Serves: 8*

🏆 **INGREDIENTS:**
- 300 g potatoes, diced
- 150 g turnip, diced
- 2 carrots, sliced
- 2 celery sticks, diced
- 1 onion, chopped
- 400 g tinned chopped tomatoes
- 500 ml vegetable stock
- 1 tsp. dried thyme
- 1 bay leaf
- Salt and pepper to taste

🍳 **DIRECTIONS:**

1. Mix all the ingredients in the Combi Pan and combine well. Slide the Combi Pan into Level 1.
2. Close the door and flip the SmartSwitch to AIR FRY/HOB. Select SLOW COOK, set temperature to HIGH and set time to 4 hours. Press START/STOP to begin cooking, until the vegetables are tender.
3. When cooking is complete, remove the pan and discard the bay leaf. Serve hot with warm bread rolls.

CHAPTER 9: SAVOURY SNACKS

Cheese and Onion Pasties

Prep Time: 20 minutes, Cook Time: 19 minutes, Serves: 4

INGREDIENTS:

- Cooking spray
- 1 sheet puff pastry
- 100 g cheddar cheese, grated
- 1 small onion, finely chopped
- 1 tbsp. olive oil
- Salt and pepper to taste

DIRECTIONS:

1. Sauté the onion with olive oil in a pan for 5 minutes, until soft and translucent. Once done, mix in the grated cheddar cheese, season with salt and pepper, and set aside to cool slightly.
2. Roll out the puff pastry and cut into 4 squares. Place the cheese and onion mixture in the centre of each square and fold to form a pasty. Seal the edges with a fork.
3. Place the Crisper Plate in the Combi Pan and set aside.
4. Close the door and flip the SmartSwitch to AIR FRY/HOB.
5. Select AIR FRY, set the temperature to 180°C and set the time to 19 minutes. Press START/STOP to begin preheating (The unit will preheat for 5 minutes).
6. While the unit is preheating, lightly spray the Crisper Plate with cooking spray and place the prepared pasties on it.
7. When 14 minutes remain on the timer, open the door and slide the pan into Level 1. Close the door to continue cooking.
8. When 7 minutes remain, open the door and flip the pasties. Close the door to continue cooking.
9. When cooking is complete, remove the pan and serve the cheese and onion pasties.

Breadcrumbs Stuffed Mushrooms

Prep: 10 minutes, Total Cook Time: 16 minutes, Steam: approx. 8 minutes, Cook: 8 minutes, Serves: 4

INGREDIENTS:

- 8 large mushrooms, stems removed
- 100 g cream cheese
- 50 g grated cheddar cheese
- 1 tbsp. fresh parsley, chopped
- 1 tbsp. breadcrumbs
- Salt and pepper to taste
- 120 ml water, for steaming

DIRECTIONS:

1. In a bowl, combine the cream cheese, grated cheddar, parsley, breadcrumbs, salt, and pepper.
2. Stuff each mushroom cap with the cheese mixture.
3. Pour 120 ml water in the Combi Pan for steaming, then slide the pan into Level 1.
4. Arrange the stuffed mushrooms on the Bake Tray. Slide tray into Level 2.
5. Close the door and flip the SmartSwitch to COMBI COOKER. Select COMBI CRISP, set the temperature to 180°C, and set the time to 8 minutes. Press START/STOP to begin cooking (The unit will steam for 8 minutes before crisping).
6. When cooking is complete, remove the tray and serve the stuffed mushrooms.

Spicy Crispy Chickpeas

🕐 *Prep Time: 5 minutes, Cook Time: 15 minutes, Serves: 4*

🏆 **INGREDIENTS:**
- 1 tin (400 g) chickpeas, drained and rinsed
- 1 tbsp. olive oil
- 1 tsp. smoked paprika
- ½ tsp. ground cumin
- ½ tsp. chilli powder
- Salt to taste

👨‍🍳 **DIRECTIONS:**
1. Place the Crisper Plate in the Combi Pan and set aside.
2. Close the door and flip the SmartSwitch to AIR FRY/HOB.
3. Select AIR FRY, set the temperature to 200°C and set the time to 20 minutes. Press START/STOP to begin preheating (The unit will preheat for 5 minutes).
4. While the unit is preheating, toss the chickpeas with olive oil, smoked paprika, cumin, chilli powder, and salt in a bowl. Place the chickpeas onto the Crisper Plate.
5. When 15 minutes remain on the timer, open the door and slide the pan into Level 1. Close the door to continue cooking.
6. When 7 minutes remain, open the door and toss the chickpeas. Close the door to continue cooking.
7. When cooking is complete, remove the pan and serve the spicy chickpeas.

Cheesy Cauliflower Bites

🕐 *Prep Time: 10 minutes, Cook Time: 12 minutes, Serves: 4*

🏆 **INGREDIENTS:**
- Cooking spray
- 1 medium cauliflower, cut into florets
- 1 egg, beaten
- 100 g grated cheddar cheese
- 100 g breadcrumbs
- 1 tbsp. olive oil
- ½ tsp. garlic powder
- Salt and pepper to taste

👨‍🍳 **DIRECTIONS:**
1. Dip the cauliflower florets into the beaten egg, then coat them in a mixture of breadcrumbs, grated cheddar cheese, olive oil, garlic powder, salt, and pepper.
2. Place the Crisper Plate in the Combi Pan and set aside.
3. Close the door and flip the SmartSwitch to AIR FRY/HOB.
4. Select AIR FRY, set the temperature to 200°C and set the time to 17 minutes. Press START/STOP to begin preheating (The unit will preheat for 5 minutes).
5. While the unit is preheating, lightly spray the Crisper Plate with cooking spray and place the breaded cauliflower on it.
6. When 12 minutes remain on the timer, open the door and slide the pan into Level 1. Close the door to continue cooking.
7. When 6 minutes remain, open the door and toss the bites. Close the door to continue cooking.
8. When cooking is complete, remove the pan and serve the cauliflower bites.

Mini Fishcakes

🕐 *Prep: 15 minutes, Total Cook Time: 18 minutes, Steam: approx. 6 minutes, Cook: 12 minutes, Serves: 4*

🍴 **INGREDIENTS:**

- Cooking spray
- 200 g white fish fillets (e.g. cod or haddock), cooked and flaked
- 100 g mashed potatoes
- 1 small onion, finely chopped
- 1 egg, beaten
- 50 g breadcrumbs
- 1 tbsp. fresh parsley, chopped
- Salt and pepper to taste
- 120 ml water, for steaming

🍳 **DIRECTIONS:**

1. In a bowl, combine the flaked fish, mashed potatoes, onion, parsley, salt, and pepper. Form into small cakes.
2. Dip each fishcake into the beaten egg, then coat with breadcrumbs. Lightly spray with cooking spray.
3. Pour 120 ml water in the Combi Pan for steaming, then slide the pan into Level 1.
4. Arrange the fishcakes on the Bake Tray. Slide tray into Level 2.
5. Close the door and flip the SmartSwitch to COMBI COOKER. Select COMBI CRISP, set the temperature to 190°C, and set the time to 12 minutes. Press START/STOP to begin cooking (The unit will steam for 6 minutes before crisping).
6. When 6 minutes remain, open the door and flip the fishcakes. Close the door to continue cooking.
7. When cooking is complete, remove the tray and serve the mini fishcakes.

Garlic Potato Wedges with Rosemary

🕐 *Prep: 10 minutes, Total Cook Time: 28 minutes, Steam: approx. 10 minutes, Cook: 18 minutes, Serves: 4*

🍴 **INGREDIENTS:**

- 1 tbsp. olive oil
- 4 medium potatoes, cut into wedges
- 2 cloves garlic, minced
- 1 tbsp. fresh rosemary, chopped
- Salt and pepper to taste
- 120 ml water, for steaming

🍳 **DIRECTIONS:**

1. In a bowl, toss the potato wedges with olive oil, minced garlic, rosemary, salt, and pepper.
2. Pour 120 ml water in the Combi Pan for steaming, then slide the pan into Level 1.
3. Arrange the seasoned wedges on the Bake Tray. Slide tray into Level 2.
4. Close the door and flip the SmartSwitch to COMBI COOKER. Select COMBI CRISP, set the temperature to 205°C, and set the time to 18 minutes. Press START/STOP to begin cooking (The unit will steam for 10 minutes before crisping).
5. When 9 minutes remain, open the door and toss the wedges. Close the door to continue cooking.
6. When cooking is complete, remove the tray and serve the potato wedges.

Crispy Fish Fingers

🕐 *Prep Time: 15 minutes, Cook Time: 10 minutes, Serves: 4*

🍴 **INGREDIENTS:**

- Cooking spray
- 4 white fish fillets (such as cod or haddock), cut into strips
- 100 g breadcrumbs
- 50 g flour
- 1 large egg, beaten
- 1 tbsp. lemon zest
- Salt and pepper to taste

🍳 **DIRECTIONS:**

1. Season the fish strips with salt, pepper, and lemon zest. Dredge the fish first in flour, then dip in the beaten egg, and finally coat with breadcrumbs.
2. Place the Crisper Plate in the Combi Pan and set aside.
3. Close the door and flip the SmartSwitch to AIR FRY/HOB.
4. Select AIR FRY, set the temperature to 200°C and set the time to 15 minutes. Press START/STOP to begin preheating (The unit will preheat for 5 minutes).
5. While the unit is preheating, lightly spray the Crisper Plate with cooking spray and place the prepared fish fingers on it.
6. When 10 minutes remain on the timer, open the door and slide the pan into Level 1. Close the door to continue cooking.
7. When 5 minutes remain, open the door and flip the fish fingers. Close the door to continue cooking.
8. When cooking is complete, remove the pan and serve the fish fingers with your favourite dipping sauce.

Garlic Mushrooms

🕐 *Prep Time: 10 minutes, Cook Time: 12 minutes, Serves: 4*

🍴 **INGREDIENTS:**

- 200 g button mushrooms, cleaned
- 1 tbsp. olive oil
- 1 tsp. garlic powder
- Salt and pepper to taste
- Fresh parsley, chopped

🍳 **DIRECTIONS:**

1. Place the Crisper Plate in the Combi Pan and set aside.
2. Close the door and flip the SmartSwitch to AIR FRY/HOB.
3. Select AIR FRY, set the temperature to 200°C and set the time to 17 minutes. Press START/STOP to begin preheating (The unit will preheat for 5 minutes).
4. While the unit is preheating, toss the mushrooms with olive oil, garlic powder, salt, and pepper in a bowl. Place the mushrooms onto the Crisper Plate.
5. When 12 minutes remain on the timer, open the door and slide the pan into Level 1. Close the door to continue cooking.
6. When 6 minutes remain, open the door and toss the mushrooms. Close the door to continue cooking.
7. When cooking is complete, remove the pan and garnish with chopped parsley before serving.

Homemade Chicken Goujons

🕐 *Prep Time: 15 minutes, Cook Time: 10 minutes, Serves: 4*

🍸 **INGREDIENTS:**

- Cooking spray
- 2 boneless, skinless chicken breasts, cut into strips
- 1 egg, beaten
- 100 g plain flour
- 100 g breadcrumbs
- 1 tsp. garlic powder
- 1 tsp. paprika
- Salt and pepper to taste

🍽 **DIRECTIONS:**

1. Dip the chicken strips into the flour, then into the beaten egg, and finally coat with breadcrumbs seasoned with garlic powder, paprika, salt, and pepper.
2. Place the Crisper Plate in the Combi Pan and set aside.
3. Close the door and flip the SmartSwitch to AIR FRY/HOB.
4. Select AIR FRY, set the temperature to 200°C and set the time to 15 minutes. Press START/STOP to begin preheating (The unit will preheat for 5 minutes).
5. While the unit is preheating, lightly spray the Crisper Plate with cooking spray and place the prepared goujons on it.
8. When 10 minutes remain on the timer, open the door and slide the pan into Level 1. Close the door to continue cooking.
6. When 5 minutes remain, open the door and flip the goujons. Close the door to continue cooking.
7. When cooking is complete, remove the pan and serve the chicken goujons.

Mushroom Arancini

🕐 *Prep: 20 minutes, Total Cook Time: 21 minutes, Steam: approx. 6 minutes, Cook: 15 minutes, Serves: 4*

🍸 **INGREDIENTS:**

- Cooking spray
- 150 g risotto rice, cooked and cooled
- 100 g mushrooms, finely chopped
- 50 g mozzarella cheese, cut into small cubes
- 1 tbsp. olive oil
- 1 egg, beaten
- 50 g breadcrumbs
- Salt and pepper to taste
- 120 ml water, for steaming

🍽 **DIRECTIONS:**

1. In a pan, heat the olive oil and sauté the mushrooms until soft, about 5 minutes.
2. Mix the cooked risotto rice with the sautéed mushrooms, salt, and pepper. Form the mixture into small balls, placing a cube of mozzarella in the centre of each ball.
3. Dip each arancini ball in the beaten egg, then coat with breadcrumbs. Lightly spray with cooking spray.
4. Pour 120 ml water in the Combi Pan for steaming, then slide the pan into Level 1.
5. Arrange the arancini on the Bake Tray. Slide tray into Level 2.
6. Close the door and flip the SmartSwitch to COMBI COOKER. Select COMBI CRISP, set the temperature to 200°C, and set the time to 10 minutes. Press START/STOP to begin cooking (The unit will steam for 6 minutes before crisping).
7. When 5 minutes remain, open the door and flip the arancini. Close the door to continue cooking.
8. When cooking is complete, remove the tray and serve the mushroom arancini.

Cheese and Chive Potato Bake

Prep: 15 minutes, Total Cook Time: 22 minutes, Steam: approx. 8 minutes, Cook: 14 minutes, Serves: 4

INGREDIENTS:
- 400 g waxy potatoes, peeled and sliced thinly
- 100 ml double cream
- 50 g cheddar cheese, grated
- 1 tbsp. fresh chives, chopped
- Salt and pepper to taste
- 120 ml water, for steaming

DIRECTIONS:
1. Pour 120 ml water in the Combi Pan for steaming, then slide the pan into Level 1.
2. Arrange the potato slices on the Bake Tray. Drizzle with double cream, sprinkle with grated cheddar cheese, chopped chives, salt, and pepper. Slide tray into Level 2.
3. Close the door and flip the SmartSwitch to COMBI COOKER. Select COMBI CRISP, set temperature to 200°C and set time to 14 minutes. Press START/STOP to begin cooking (The unit will steam for 8 minutes before crisping).
4. When cooking is complete, remove the tray from the unit and serve the cheesy potato.

Mini Sausage Rolls

Prep Time: 15 minutes, Cook Time: 13 minutes, Serves: 4

INGREDIENTS:
- 250 g sausage meat
- 1 sheet puff pastry
- 1 egg, beaten (for glazing)
- 1 tsp. mustard (optional)
- Salt and pepper to taste

DIRECTIONS:
1. Roll out the puff pastry and cut it into small rectangles.
2. Place a spoonful of sausage meat along the edge of each rectangle, then roll up to form a small sausage roll. Season with salt and pepper to taste. Brush with the beaten egg and add a touch of mustard if desired.
3. Place the Crisper Plate in the Combi Pan and set aside.
4. Close the door and flip the SmartSwitch to AIR FRY/HOB.
5. Select AIR FRY, set the temperature to 190°C and set the time to 18 minutes. Press START/STOP to begin preheating (The unit will preheat for 5 minutes).
6. While the unit is preheating, place sausage rolls onto the Crisper Plate.
7. When 13 minutes remain on the timer, open the door and slide the pan into Level 1. Close the door to continue cooking.
8. When cooking is complete, remove the pan and serve the mini sausage rolls.

Apple and Cinnamon Cake

Prep: 20 minutes, Total Cook Time: 50 minutes, Steam: approx. 15 minutes, Cook: 35 minutes, Serves: 8

INGREDIENTS:

- Cooking spray
- 200 g self-raising flour
- 150 g caster sugar
- 200 g unsalted butter, softened
- 2 large eggs
- 2 medium apples, peeled, cored, and chopped
- 1 tsp. ground cinnamon
- 1 tsp. vanilla extract
- 240 ml water, for steaming

DIRECTIONS:

1. Pour 240 ml water into the Combi Pan for steaming. Place the Crisper Plate on top, then spray a 22-cm round cake pan with cooking spray. Set aside.
2. In a bowl, cream together the butter and sugar. Add the eggs one at a time, then stir in the cinnamon, vanilla extract, and flour.
3. Fold in the chopped apples and pour the batter into the greased cake pan.
4. Place the cake pan into the Combi Pan on top of the Crisper Plate. Slide the pan into Level 1.
5. Close the door and flip the SmartSwitch to COMBI COOKER. Select COMBI BAKE, set the temperature to 160°C, and set the time to 35 minutes. Press START/STOP to begin cooking. (The unit will steam for 15 minutes before baking).
6. When cooking is complete, remove the cake from the pan and allow it to cool before serving.

Banoffee Pie

Prep: 20 minutes, Total Cook Time: 60 minutes, Steam: approx. 15 minutes, Cook: 45 minutes, Serves: 8

INGREDIENTS:

- Cooking spray
- 250 g digestive biscuits, crushed
- 100 g unsalted butter, melted
- 300 g toffee sauce
- 3 ripe bananas, sliced
- 300 ml double cream, whipped
- 50 g dark chocolate, grated
- 240 ml water, for steaming

DIRECTIONS:

1. Pour 240 ml water into the Combi Pan for steaming. Place the Crisper Plate on top of the Combi Pan.
2. Spray a 22-cm round cake pan with cooking spray and set aside.
3. Combine the crushed digestive biscuits with the melted butter, and press the mixture into the bottom of the prepared cake pan to form the base.
4. Place the cake pan into the Combi Pan on top of the Crisper Plate. Slide the pan into Level 1.
5. Close the door and flip the SmartSwitch to COMBI COOKER. Select COMBI BAKE, set the temperature to 160°C, and set the time to 45 minutes. Press START/STOP to begin cooking (The unit will steam for 15 minutes before baking).
6. When the cooking is complete, remove the cake pan and allow the base to cool.
7. Once cooled, top the base with toffee sauce, sliced bananas, whipped cream, and grated dark chocolate.
8. Refrigerate the pie until fully chilled before serving.

Carrot and Walnut Cake

🕐 *Prep: 20 minutes, Total Cook Time: 55 minutes, Steam: approx. 15 minutes, Cook: 40 minutes, Serves: 8*

🍽 INGREDIENTS:

- Cooking spray
- 200 g self-raising flour
- 200 g caster sugar
- 200 g unsalted butter, softened
- 3 large eggs
- 2 large carrots, grated
- 100 g walnuts, chopped
- 1 tsp. baking powder
- 1 tsp. ground cinnamon
- 180 ml water, for steaming

🍴 DIRECTIONS:

1. Pour 180 ml water into the Combi Pan for steaming. Place the Crisper Plate on top, then spray a 22-cm round cake pan with cooking spray. Set aside.
2. In a bowl, cream together the butter and sugar. Add the eggs one at a time, mixing well after each addition.
3. Stir in the grated carrots, walnuts, baking powder, cinnamon, and self-raising flour until combined. Pour the batter into the greased cake pan.
4. Place the cake pan into the Combi Pan on top of the Crisper Plate. Slide the pan into Level 1.
5. Close the door and flip the SmartSwitch to COMBI COOKER. Select COMBI BAKE, set the temperature to 170°C, and set the time to 40 minutes. Press START/STOP to begin cooking. (The unit will steam for 15 minutes before baking).
6. When cooking is complete, remove the pan from the unit and allow the cake to cool.

Homemade Bread Rolls

🕐 *Prep: 20 minutes, Prove: 40 minutes, Total Cook Time: 40 minutes, Steam: approx. 15 minutes, Cook: 25 minutes, Serves: 10*

🍽 INGREDIENTS:

- Cooking spray
- 500 g strong white bread flour
- 10 g salt
- 10 g easy-bake yeast
- 40 g unsalted butter, softened
- 300 ml lukewarm water
- 120 ml water, for steaming

🍴 DIRECTIONS:

1. Pour 120 ml water into the Combi Pan for steaming. Place the Crisper Plate on top, then spray a 22-cm round cake pan with cooking spray. Set aside.
2. In a bowl, mix the flour, salt, and yeast. Add the butter and lukewarm water, then knead the dough for 10 minutes until smooth and elastic.
3. Spread the dough to roughly fit the prepared cake pan. Place the pan into the Combi Pan on top of the Crisper Plate. Slide the pan into Level 1.
4. Close door and flip the SmartSwitch to COMBI COOKER. Select PROVE, set temperature to 35°C and set time to 40 minutes. Press START/STOP and begin proving.
5. After proving, punch down the dough and divide it into 10 equal portions. Shape each portion into a ball and place in the prepared pan.
6. Place the pan into the Combi Pan on top of the Crisper Plate.
7. Close the door and select COMBI BAKE, set the temperature to 180°C and the time to 25 minutes. Press START/STOP to begin cooking (The unit will steam for 15 minutes before baking).
8. When cooking is complete, remove the pan from the unit and cool on a wire rack.

Sticky Toffee Pudding

🕐 Prep: 15 minutes, Total Cook Time: 45 minutes, Steam: approx. 15 minutes, Cook: 30 minutes, Serves: 6

🍯 **INGREDIENTS:**

- Cooking spray
- 200 g dates, chopped
- 200 ml boiling water
- 1 tsp. bicarbonate of soda
- 100 g unsalted butter, softened
- 100 g dark brown sugar
- 2 large eggs
- 200 g self-raising flour
- 1 tsp. vanilla extract
- 240 ml water, for steaming
- 100 ml toffee sauce, for serving

🍳 **DIRECTIONS:**

1. Pour 240 ml water into the Combi Pan for steaming. Place the Crisper Plate on top, then spray a 22-cm round cake pan with cooking spray. Set aside.
2. In a bowl, combine the chopped dates and boiling water. Add the bicarbonate of soda and stir to combine.
3. In another bowl, cream together the butter and sugar. Add the eggs and vanilla extract, then fold in the flour.
4. Stir in the date mixture and pour the batter into the greased cake pan.
5. Place the cake pan into the Combi Pan on top of the Crisper Plate. Slide the pan into Level 1.
6. Close the door and flip the SmartSwitch to COMBI COOKER. Select COMBI BAKE, set the temperature to 180°C, and set the time to 30 minutes. Press START/STOP to begin cooking. (The unit will steam for 15 minutes before baking).
7. When cooking is complete, remove the pan and allow the pudding to cool slightly. Serve warm with toffee sauce.

Gingerbread Cake

🕐 Prep Time: 15 minutes, Cook Time: 40 minutes, Serves: 8

🍯 **INGREDIENTS:**

- 250 g self-raising flour
- 100 g dark brown sugar
- 1 tsp. ground ginger
- 1 tsp. ground cinnamon
- ½ tsp. ground cloves
- 1 tsp. bicarbonate of soda
- 200 g unsalted butter, softened
- 2 large eggs
- 200 ml milk
- 2 tbsps. golden syrup

🍳 **DIRECTIONS:**

1. In a bowl, mix the flour, sugar, ginger, cinnamon, cloves, and bicarbonate of soda.
2. In another bowl, cream together the butter and eggs. Add the milk and golden syrup and mix until smooth. Gradually add the dry ingredients and stir well to combine. Transfer the mixture to the Combi Pan
3. Flip the SmartSwitch to AIR FRY/HOB. Select BAKE, set the temperature to 180°C, and set the time to 43 minutes. Press START/STOP to begin preheating (The unit will preheat for 3 minutes).
4. When preheat is complete, open the door and slide the Combi Pan into Level 1. Close the door to start cooking, until the cake is golden and a skewer inserted into the centre comes out clean.
5. When cooking is complete, pull the Combi Pan out and allow the cake to cool slightly before serving.

Chocolate Chip Cookies

🕐 *Prep Time: 10 minutes, Cook Time: 12 minutes, Serves: 12*

🍽 **INGREDIENTS:**
- 100 g unsalted butter, softened
- 100 g caster sugar
- 100 g brown sugar
- 1 large egg
- 1 tsp. vanilla extract
- 150 g plain flour
- 1 tsp. baking powder
- 100 g chocolate chips

👨‍🍳 **DIRECTIONS:**

1. Combine all the ingredients in a bowl and make a cookie dough.
2. Place the Crisper Plate in the Combi Pan and arrange the cookie dough in spoonfuls on the plate, leaving space between each.
3. Flip the SmartSwitch to AIR FRY/HOB. Select BAKE, set the temperature to 170°C, and set the time to 15 minutes. Press START/STOP to begin preheating (The unit will preheat for 3 minutes).
4. When preheat is complete, open the door and slide the pan into Level 1. Close the door to start cooking, until the cookies are golden and firm around the edges.
5. When cooking is complete, pull the Combi Pan out and allow the cookies to cool slightly before serving.

Homemade Apple Crumble

🕐 *Prep Time: 10 minutes, Cook Time: 30 minutes, Serves: 6*

🍽 **INGREDIENTS:**
- 6 medium apples, peeled and sliced
- 50 g caster sugar
- 1 tsp. ground cinnamon
- 150 g plain flour
- 100 g unsalted butter, chilled and cubed
- 75 g demerara sugar
- Custard or cream for serving

👨‍🍳 **DIRECTIONS:**

1. Add the sliced apples, caster sugar, and cinnamon to the Combi Pan and mix to combine.
2. For the crumble topping, place the flour and butter in a bowl and rub together with your fingertips until it resembles breadcrumbs. Stir in the demerara sugar.
3. Sprinkle the crumble topping over the apples in the Combi Pan.
4. Flip the SmartSwitch to AIR FRY/HOB. Select BAKE, set the temperature to 190°C, and set the time to 33 minutes. Press START/STOP to begin preheating (The unit will preheat for 3 minutes).
5. When preheat is complete, open the door and slide the Combi Pan into Level 1. Close the door to start cooking, until the crumble is golden and the apples are tender.
6. When cooking is complete, pull the Combi Pan out and serve warm with custard or cream.

Victoria Sponge Cake

🕐 *Prep Time: 15 minutes, Cook Time: 30 minutes, Serves: 8*

🏆 INGREDIENTS:

- 200 g self-raising flour
- 200 g caster sugar
- 200 g unsalted butter, softened
- 4 large eggs
- 1 tsp. vanilla extract
- 2 tbsps. milk
- 150 g strawberry jam
- Icing sugar for dusting

🍳 DIRECTIONS:

1. Add the flour, sugar, butter, eggs, vanilla extract, and milk to the Combi Pan and stir well to combine.
2. Flip the SmartSwitch to AIR FRY/HOB. Select BAKE, set the temperature to 180°C, and set the time to 33 minutes. Press START/STOP to begin preheating (The unit will preheat for 3 minutes).
3. When preheat is complete, open the door and slide the Combi Pan into Level 1. Close the door to start cooking, until the cake is golden brown and a skewer inserted into the centre comes out clean.
4. When cooking is complete, carefully remove the Combi Pan and allow the cake to cool in the pan for 10-15 minutes. Then transfer the cake onto a wire rack to cool completely.
5. Once the cake has cooled completely, slice it horizontally into two even layers using a serrated knife.
6. Spread the strawberry jam evenly over the top surface of the bottom layer. Place the second layer on top and gently press down to secure.
7. Dust the top of the cake with icing sugar before serving.

Cinnamon Buns

🕐 *Prep: 20 minutes, Prove: 40 minutes, Total Cook Time: 40 minutes, Steam: approx. 15 minutes, Cook: 25 minutes, Serves: 10*

🏆 INGREDIENTS:

- Cooking spray
- 300 g strong white flour
- 50 g caster sugar
- 1 tsp. easy-bake yeast
- 1 tsp. salt
- 60 g unsalted butter, melted, divided
- 200 ml whole milk
- 1 large egg
- 100 g brown sugar
- 2 tsp. ground cinnamon
- 120 ml water, for steaming

🍳 DIRECTIONS:

1. Pour 120 ml water into the Combi Pan for steaming. Place the Crisper Plate on top, then spray a 22-cm round cake pan with cooking spray. Set aside.
2. In a bowl, mix the flour, caster sugar, yeast, and salt. Add 40 g melted butter, warm milk, and egg. Mix to form a dough.
3. Spread the dough to roughly fit the prepared cake pan. Place the pan into the Combi Pan on top of the Crisper Plate. Slide the pan into Level 1.
4. Close door and flip the SmartSwitch to COMBI COOKER. Select PROVE, set temperature to 35°C and set time to 40 minutes. Press START/STOP and begin proving.
5. Once the dough has proved, roll it out on a lightly floured surface into a rectangle. Spread with the remaining butter and sprinkle with cinnamon and brown sugar. Roll the dough up tightly and cut into 10 slices.
6. Place the slices into the prepared cake pan. Place the pan into the Combi Pan on top of the Crisper Plate.
7. Close the door and select COMBI BAKE, set the temperature to 180°C and the time to 25 minutes. Press START/STOP to begin cooking (The unit will steam for 15 minutes before baking).
8. When cooking is complete, remove the pan from the unit. Allow to cool before icing, if desired.

Treacle Tart

🕐 *Prep: 20 minutes, Total Cook Time: 50 minutes, Steam: approx. 15 minutes, Cook: 35 minutes, Serves: 8*

🏆 **INGREDIENTS:**

- Cooking spray
- 250 g shortcrust pastry
- 300 g golden syrup
- 100 g breadcrumbs
- 50 g double cream
- 1 tbsp. lemon juice
- 240 ml water, for steaming

👨‍🍳 **DIRECTIONS:**

1. Pour 240 ml water into the Combi Pan for steaming. Place the Crisper Plate on top, then spray a 22-cm round cake pan with cooking spray. Set aside.
2. Roll out the shortcrust pastry and line the cake pan with it.
3. In a bowl, combine the golden syrup, breadcrumbs, double cream, and lemon juice. Pour this mixture into the pastry-lined cake pan.
4. Place the cake pan into the Combi Pan on top of the Crisper Plate. Slide the pan into Level 1.
5. Close the door and flip the SmartSwitch to COMBI COOKER. Select COMBI BAKE, set the temperature to 180°C, and set the time to 35 minutes. Press START/STOP to begin cooking. (The unit will steam for 15 minutes before baking.)
6. When cooking is complete, remove the pan and allow the tart to cool before serving with a dollop of clotted cream.

Fruit Loaf Cake

🕐 *Prep: 20 minutes, Prove: 40 minutes, Total Cook Time: 1 hour, Steam: approx. 15 minutes, Cook: 45 minutes, Serves: 8*

🏆 **INGREDIENTS:**

- Cooking spray
- 300 g mixed dried fruit (raisins, sultanas, currants)
- 250 g self-raising flour
- 100 g brown sugar
- 1 tsp. mixed spice powder
- 1 tsp. ground cinnamon
- 1 egg
- 200 ml whole milk
- 50 g unsalted butter, melted
- 120 ml water, for steaming

👨‍🍳 **DIRECTIONS:**

1. Pour 120 ml water into the Combi Pan for steaming. Place the Crisper Plate on top, then spray a 22-cm round cake pan with cooking spray. Set aside.
2. In a bowl, mix the flour, sugar, mixed spice powder, and cinnamon. Add the milk, egg, and melted butter, and stir until combined.
3. Fold in the dried fruit. Place the mixture into the prepared cake pan. Place the pan into the Combi Pan on top of the Crisper Plate. Slide the pan into Level 1.
4. Close door and flip the SmartSwitch to COMBI COOKER. Select PROVE, set temperature to 35°C and set time to 40 minutes. Press START/STOP and begin proving.
5. After proving, close the door and select COMBI BAKE, set the temperature to 170°C and set the time to 45 minutes. Press START/STOP to begin cooking (The unit will steam for 15 minutes before baking).
6. When cooking is complete, remove the pan from the unit and cool before serving.

Appendix 1:
Measurement Conversion Chart

WEIGHT EQUIVALENTS

METRIC	US STANDARD	US STANDARD (OUNCES)
15 g	1 tablespoon	1/2 ounce
30 g	1/8 cup	1 ounce
60 g	1/4 cup	2 ounces
115 g	1/2 cup	4 ounces
170 g	3/4 cup	6 ounces
225 g	1 cup	8 ounces
450 g	2 cups	16 ounces
900 g	4 cups	2 pounds

VOLUME EQUIVALENTS

METRIC	US STANDARD	US STANDARD (OUNCES)
15 ml	1 tablespoon	1/2 fl.oz.
30 ml	2 tablespoons	1 fl.oz.
60 ml	1/4 cup	2 fl.oz.
125 ml	1/2 cup	4 fl.oz.
180 ml	3/4 cup	6 fl.oz.
250 ml	1 cup	8 fl.oz.
500 ml	2 cups	16 fl.oz.
1000 ml	4 cups	1 quart

TEMPERATURES EQUIVALENTS

CELSIUS (C)	FAHRENHEIT (F) (APPROXIMATE)
120 °C	250 °F
135 °C	275 °F
150 °C	300 °F
160 °C	325 °F
175 °C	350 °F
190 °C	375 °F
205 °C	400 °F
220 °C	425 °F
230 °C	450 °F
245°C	475 °F
260 °C	500 °F

LENGTH EQUIVALENTS

METRIC	IMPERIAL
3 mm	1/8 inch
6 mm	1/4 inch
1 cm	1/2 inch
2.5 cm	1 inch
3 cm	1 1/4 inches
5 cm	2 inches
10 cm	4 inches
15 cm	6 inches
20 cm	8 inches

Appendix 2:
Recipes Index

A

Apple

Apple and Cinnamon Cake / 60

Homemade Apple Crumble / 63

Asparagus

Roasted Asparagus with Lemon and
   Parmesan / 35

Avocado

Avocado and Egg Toast / 13

B

Bacon

Pigs in Blankets / 48

Banana

Banoffee Pie / 60

Beef

Beef and Broccoli Meal / 19

Spaghetti Bolognese / 19

Beef and Ale Stew / 32

Grilled Beef Burgers with Cheddar Cheese / 48

Beef Brisket

Beef Brisket with Horseradish Sauce / 34

Beef Fillet

Beef Wellington Bites / 53

Beef Steak

Beef and Mushroom Stroganoff with Egg
   Noodles / 24

Steak and Kidney Pie / 49

Beetroot

Beetroot with Feta and Walnuts / 38

Broccoli

Vegetable Mac and Cheese / 24

Steamed Garlic Butter Broccoli / 35

Button Mushroom

Buttery Mushrooms with Garlic and Thyme / 40

Garlic Mushrooms / 57

C

Carrot

Honey Glazed Roast Carrots with Mustard
   Seeds / 39

Carrot and Walnut Cake / 61

Cauliflower

Mustard Cauliflower with Cheddar / 37

Cheesy Cauliflower Bites / 55

Chicken Breast

Chicken Alfredo Pasta / 18

Mediterranean Chicken with Couscous / 28

Stuffed Chicken Breast with Spinach and Feta / 29

Homemade Chicken Goujons / 58

Chicken Drumstick

Chicken and Pesto Pasta / 20

Chicken Thigh

Chicken and Pea Risotto / 27

Sticky Chicken Thighs with Honey and
   Mustard / 32

Chickpea

Chickpea and Spinach Stir-Fry / 37

Spicy Crispy Chickpeas / 55

Chocolate Chip

Chocolate Chip Cookies / 63

Cod

Baked Cod with Parsley Crust / 46

Courgette

Grilled Halloumi and Vegetable Skewers / 33

Crispy Parmesan Courgettes / 36

Crab

Crab Cakes with Lemon and Dill / 44

D

Date

Sticky Toffee Pudding / 62

Dried Fruit

Fruit Loaf Cake / 65

Duck Breast

Crispy Duck Breast with Orange Sauce / 30

H

Haddock

Traditional Steamed Haddock with Peas / 45

Ham

Grilled Cheese and Ham Toastie / 12

Pea and Ham Rice Pilaf / 22

K

Kidney Bean

Spicy Chilli Rice / 27

L

Lamb

Lamb Kofta and Couscous / 18

Classic Shepherd's Pie / 52

Lamb Chop

Lamb Chops with Garlic and Thyme / 50

Lamb Shoulder

Traditional Lamb Hotpot / 33

Lamb Steak

Grilled Lamb Steak with Basil Pasta / 28

Leek

Creamy Potato and Leek Soup / 38

Leg Of Lamb

Herb-Crusted Leg of Lamb / 29

Lemon

Lemon and Herb Rice Pilaf / 26

Lobster Tail

Lobster Tails with Herbed Butter / 42

M

Mushroom

Breadcrumbs Stuffed Mushrooms / 54

Mushroom Arancini / 58

Mussel

Mussels and Garlic Pasta / 20

Mussels in Garlic Butter / 43

O

Onion

Cheese and Onion Pasties / 54

Oyster

Grilled Garlic Oysters with Parsley / 43

P

Pork Belly

Crispy Pork Belly with Apple Sauce / 51

Pork Chop

Pork Chop and Pumpkin Linguine / 21

Pork Tenderloin

Sweet and Sour Pork with Rice / 25

Seared Pork Tenderloin with Apple and Sage / 31

Potato

Slow Cooked Breakfast Casserole / 14

Vegetarian Breakfast Hash / 16

Steamed Minted New Potatoes / 40

Classic British Vegetable Stew / 53

Garlic Potato Wedges with Rosemary / 56

Cheese and Chive Potato Bake / 59

Prawn

Prawn and Tomato Pasta / 25

Grilled Prawn Skewers with Lime and
    Coriander / 41

Battered Prawns with Garlic Mayonnaise / 42

Pumpkin

Roasted Pumpkin with Sage and Nutmeg / 36

R

Red Pepper

Meatball and Peppers Pasta / 26

Rib-Eye Steak

Grilled Rib-eye Steak with Garlic Butter / 30

S

Salmon

Salmon and Leek with Quinoa / 17

Salmon and Spinach Risotto / 23

Steamed Lemon Herb Salmon / 41

Salmon Stir-Fry with Asparagus and Spinach / 44

Sausage

Classic Full English Breakfast / 11

Toad in the Hole / 14

Sausage and Mushroom Breakfast Casserole / 16

Bangers and Mash with Onion Gravy / 31

Classic Scotch Eggs / 47

Stuffing Balls / 50

Mini Sausage Rolls / 59

Scallop

Chilli Scallops with Coriander / 46

Seafood

Creamy Seafood Pasta / 23

Sirloin Steak

Beef Steak and Spinach Pasta / 17

Sweet Potato

Thyme Sweet Potato Wedges / 39

T

Tofu

Thai Red Curry with Tofu and Rice / 21

Tomato

Grilled Bacon and Tomato Sandwich / 15

Creamy Tomato and Basil Rice / 22

W

White Fish

Fish and Chips / 49

Mini Fishcakes / 56

Crispy Fish Fingers / 57

Whole Chicken

Classic Roast Chicken with Root Vegetables / 34

Whole Trout

Grilled Whole Trout with Lemon / 45

HERE ARE YOUR FREE BONUSES:

NINJA COMBI MULTICOOKER INSPIRATION GUIDE
NINJA COMBI MULTICOOKER INSTRUCTION BOOKLET

Paperback PDF

STEP 1: POST A QUICK REVIEW

Qualify to receive the 3 free Bonuses by posting a **SUPER QUICK** review on **AMAZON.CO.UK** (Optional, but I'd really love to get your Feedback)

POST A REVIEW

or Scan the QR code to Review

STEP 2: GET YOUR QUALIFY

Send your review record to me by QR CODE

STEP 3 DOWNLOAD YOUR FREE BONUSES

Quick Start Guide

User Manual

Ebook PDF

Printed in Dunstable, United Kingdom

72006010R00045